MOS 2013 Study Guide
for Microsoft PowerPoint

Joan Lambert

PUBLISHED BY
Microsoft Press
A Division of Microsoft Corporation
One Microsoft Way
Redmond, Washington 98052-6399

Library of Congress Control Number: 2013941816
ISBN: 978-0-7356-6923-9

Printed and bound in the United States of America.

First Printing

Microsoft Press books are available through booksellers and distributors worldwide. If you need support related to this book, email Microsoft Press Book Support at mspinput@microsoft.com. Please tell us what you think of this book at http://www.microsoft.com/learning/booksurvey.

Microsoft and the trademarks listed at http://www.microsoft.com/en-us/legal/intellectualproperty/trademarks/en-us.aspx are trademarks of the Microsoft group of companies. All other marks are property of their respective owners.

The example companies, organizations, products, domain names, email addresses, logos, people, places, and events depicted herein are fictitious. No association with any real company, organization, product, domain name, email address, logo, person, place, or event is intended or should be inferred.

This book expresses the author's views and opinions. The information contained in this book is provided without any express, statutory, or implied warranties. Neither the authors, Microsoft Corporation, nor its resellers, or distributors will be held liable for any damages caused or alleged to be caused either directly or indirectly by this book.

Acquisitions Editor: Rosemary Caperton
Editorial Production: Online Training Solutions, Inc. (OTSI)
Technical Reviewer: Rob Carr (OTSI)
Copyeditor: Kathy Krause (OTSI)
Indexer: Krista Wall (OTSI)
Cover: Microsoft Press Brand Team

Contents

What do you think of this book? We want to hear from you!

Microsoft is interested in hearing your feedback so we can continually improve our books and learning resources for you. To participate in a brief online survey, please visit:

> microsoft.com/learning/booksurvey

What do you think of this book? We want to hear from you!

Microsoft is interested in hearing your feedback so we can continually improve our books and learning resources for you. To participate in a brief online survey, please visit:

microsoft.com/learning/booksurvey

Introduction

The Microsoft Office Specialist (MOS) certification program has been designed to validate your knowledge of and ability to use programs in the Microsoft Office 2013 suite of programs, Microsoft Office 365, and Microsoft SharePoint. This book has been designed to guide you in studying the types of tasks you are likely to be required to demonstrate in Exam 77-422: Microsoft PowerPoint 2013.

Who this book is for

MOS 2013 Study Guide for Microsoft PowerPoint is designed for experienced computer users seeking Microsoft Office Specialist certification in PowerPoint 2013.

The MOS exams for individual programs are practical rather than theoretical. You must demonstrate that you can complete certain tasks or projects rather than simply answering questions about program features. The successful MOS certification candidate will have at least six months of experience using all aspects of the application on a regular basis— for example, using PowerPoint at work or school to create and manage presentations and slides, insert and format slide content (including shapes, text, tables, charts, SmartArt graphics, images, and media), animate slide content, transition between slides, manage multiple versions of a presentation, and prepare presentations for delivery.

As a certification candidate, you probably have a lot of experience with the program you want to become certified in. Many of the procedures described in this book will be familiar to you; others might not be. Read through each study section and ensure that you are familiar with not only the procedures included in the section, but also the concepts and tools discussed in the review information. In some cases, graphics depict the tools you will use to perform procedures related to the skill set. Study the graphics and ensure that you are familiar with all the options available for each tool.

How this book is organized

The exam coverage is divided into chapters representing broad skill sets that correlate to the functional groups covered by the exam, and each chapter is divided into sections addressing groups of related skills that correlate to the exam objectives. Each section includes review information, generic procedures, and practice tasks you can complete on your own while studying. When necessary, we provide practice files you can use to work through the practice tasks. You can practice the procedures in this book by using the practice files supplied or by using your own files.

Download the practice files

Before you can complete the practice tasks in this book, you need to download the book's practice files to your computer. These practice files can be downloaded from the following page:

http://aka.ms/mosPowerPoint2013/files

> **Important** The PowerPoint 2013 program is not available from this website. You should purchase and install that program before using this book.

If you would like to be able to refer to the completed versions of practice files at a later time, you can save the practice files that you modify while working through the practice tasks in this book. If you save your changes and later want to repeat the practice task, you can download the original practice files again.

The following table lists the practice files for this book.

Folder and chapter	Files
MOSPowerPoint2013\Objective1 1 Create and manage presentations	*PowerPoint_1-1a.txt*
	PowerPoint_1-1b.docx
	PowerPoint_1-2a.pptx
	PowerPoint_1-2b.pptx
	PowerPoint_1-2c.png
	PowerPoint_1-3.pptx
	PowerPoint_1-4a.pptx
	PowerPoint_1-4b.pptx
	PowerPoint_1-5.pptx

Folder and chapter	Files
MOSPowerPoint2013\Objective2 2 Insert and format slides and shapes	*PowerPoint_2-1.pptx* *PowerPoint_2-2.pptx* *PowerPoint_2-3.pptx*
MOSPowerPoint2013\Objective3 3 Create slide content	*PowerPoint_3-1.pptx* *PowerPoint_3-2a.pptx* *PowerPoint_3-2b.xlsx* *PowerPoint_3-3a.pptx* *PowerPoint_3-3b.xlsx* *PowerPoint_3-3c.pptx* *PowerPoint_3-4.pptx* *PowerPoint_3-5.pptx* *PowerPoint_3-6a.pptx* *PowerPoint_3-6b.mp4*
MOSPowerPoint2013\Objective4 4 Apply transitions and animations	*PowerPoint_4-1a.pptx* *PowerPoint_4-1b.pptx* *PowerPoint_4-2.pptx* *PowerPoint_4-3.pptx*
MOSPowerPoint2013\Objective5 5 Manage multiple presentations	*PowerPoint_5-1a.pptx* *PowerPoint_5-1b.pptx* *PowerPoint_5-2a.pptx* *PowerPoint_5-2b.pptx* *PowerPoint_5-2c.pptx* *PowerPoint_5-2d.pptx* *PowerPoint_5-3a.pptx* *PowerPoint_5-3b.pptx*

Adapting exercise steps

The screen images shown in this book were captured at a screen resolution of 1024 × 768, at 100 percent magnification. If your settings are different, the ribbon on your screen might not look the same as the one shown in this book. For example, you might have more or fewer buttons in each of the groups, the buttons you have might be represented by larger or smaller icons than those shown, or the group might be represented by a button that you click to display the group's commands. As a result, exercise instructions that involve the ribbon might require a little adaptation. Our instructions use this format:

- On the **Insert** tab, in the **Illustrations** group, click the **Chart** button.

If the command is in a list or on a menu, our instructions use this format:

- On the **Home** tab, in the **Editing** group, click the **Find** arrow, and then click **Advanced Find**.

> **Tip** On subsequent instances of instructions located on the same tab or in the same group, the instructions are simplified to reflect that we've already established the working location.

If differences between your display settings and ours cause a button to appear differently on your screen from the way it does in this book, you can easily adapt the steps to locate the command. First click the specified tab, and then locate the specified group. If a group has been collapsed into a group list or under a group button, click the list or button to display the group's commands. If you can't immediately identify the button you want, point to likely candidates to display their names in ScreenTips.

If you prefer not to have to adapt the steps, set up your screen to match ours while you read and work through the exercises in this book.

In this book, we provide instructions based on the traditional keyboard and mouse input methods. If you're using the program on a touch-enabled device, you might be giving commands by tapping with a stylus or your finger. If so, substitute a tapping action any time we instruct you to click a user interface element. Also note that when we tell you to enter information, you can do so by typing on a keyboard, tapping an on-screen keyboard, or even speaking aloud, depending on your computer setup and your personal preferences.

Ebook edition

If you're reading the ebook edition of this book, you can do the following:

- Search the full text
- Print
- Copy and paste

You can purchase and download the ebook edition from:
http://aka.ms/mosPowerPoint2013

Get support and give feedback

The following sections provide information about getting help with this book and contacting us to provide feedback or report errors.

Errata

We've made every effort to ensure the accuracy of this book and its companion content. Any errors that have been reported since this book was published are listed at:

http://aka.ms/mosPowerPoint2013/errata

If you find an error that is not already listed, you can report it to us through the same page.

If you need additional support, send an email message to Microsoft Press Book Support at:

mspinput@microsoft.com

Please note that product support for Microsoft software is not offered through the preceding addresses.

We want to hear from you

At Microsoft Press, your satisfaction is our top priority, and your feedback our most valuable asset. Please tell us what you think of this book at:

http://www.microsoft.com/learning/booksurvey

The survey is short, and we read every one of your comments and ideas. Thanks in advance for your input!

Stay in touch

Let's keep the conversation going! We're on Twitter at:

http://twitter.com/MicrosoftPress

Taking a Microsoft Office Specialist exam

Desktop computing proficiency is increasingly important in today's business world. When screening, hiring, and training employees, employers can feel reassured by relying on the objectivity and consistency of technology certification to ensure the competence of their workforce. As an employee or job seeker, you can use technology certification to prove that you already have the skills you need to succeed, saving current and future employers the time and expense of training you.

Microsoft Office Specialist certification

Microsoft Office Specialist certification is designed to assist employees in validating their skills with Office programs. The following certification paths are available:

- A Microsoft Office Specialist (MOS) is an individual who has demonstrated proficiency by passing a certification exam in one or more Office programs, including Microsoft Word, Excel, PowerPoint, Outlook, Access, OneNote, or SharePoint.

- A Microsoft Office Specialist Expert (MOS Expert) is an individual who has demonstrated that he or she has mastered the more advanced features of Word or Excel by passing the required certification exams.

- A Microsoft Office Specialist Master (MOS Master) is an individual who has demonstrated that he or she has mastered multiple Office applications by passing the MOS Expert certification exams for Word and Excel, the MOS certification exam for PowerPoint, and one additional MOS certification exam.

Choosing a certification path

When deciding which certifications you would like to pursue, you should assess the following:

- The program and program versions with which you are familiar
- The length of time you have used the program and how frequently you use it
- Whether you have had formal or informal training in the use of that program
- Whether you use most or all of the available program features
- Whether you are considered a go-to resource by business associates, friends, and family members who have difficulty with the program

Candidates for MOS-level certification are expected to successfully complete a wide range of standard business tasks, such as formatting a document or worksheet and its content; creating and formatting visual content; or working with SharePoint lists, libraries, Web Parts, and dashboards. Successful candidates generally have six or more months of experience with the specific Office program, including either formal, instructor-led training or self-study using MOS-approved books, guides, or interactive computer-based materials.

Candidates for MOS Expert–level certification are expected to successfully complete more complex tasks that involve using the advanced functionality of the program. Successful candidates generally have at least six months, and may have several years, of experience with the programs, including formal, instructor-led training or self-study using MOS-approved materials.

Test-taking tips

Every MOS certification exam is developed from a set of exam skill standards (referred to as the *objective domain*) that are derived from studies of how the Office programs are used in the workplace. Because these skill standards dictate the scope of each exam, they provide critical information about how to prepare for certification. This book follows the structure of the published exam objectives; see "How this book is organized" in the Introduction for more information.

The MOS certification exams are performance based and require you to complete business-related tasks or projects in the program for which you are seeking certification. For example, you might be presented with a file and told to do something specific with it, or presented with a sample document and told to create it by using resources provided for that purpose. Your score on the exam reflects how well you perform the requested tasks or complete the project within the allotted time.

Here is some helpful information about taking the exam:

- Keep track of the time. Your exam time does not officially begin until after you finish reading the instructions provided at the beginning of the exam. During the exam, the amount of time remaining is shown at the bottom of the exam interface. You can't pause the exam after you start it.

- Pace yourself. At the beginning of the exam, you will receive information about the questions or projects that are included in the exam. Some questions will require that you complete more than one task. Each project will require that you complete multiple tasks. During the exam, the amount of time remaining to complete the questions or project, and the number of completed and remaining questions if applicable, is shown at the bottom of the exam interface.

- Read the exam instructions carefully before beginning. Follow all the instructions provided completely and accurately.

- Enter requested information as it appears in the instructions, but without duplicating the formatting unless you are specifically instructed to do so. For example, the text and values you are asked to enter might appear in the instructions in bold and underlined text, but you should enter the information without applying these formats.

- Close all dialog boxes before proceeding to the next exam question unless you are specifically instructed not to do so.

- Don't close task panes before proceeding to the next exam question unless you are specifically instructed to do so.

- If you are asked to print a document, worksheet, chart, report, or slide, perform the task, but be aware that nothing will actually be printed.

- When performing tasks to complete a project-based exam, save your work frequently.

- Don't worry about extra keystrokes or mouse clicks. Your work is scored based on its result, not on the method you use to achieve that result (unless a specific method is indicated in the instructions).

- If a computer problem occurs during the exam (for example, if the exam does not respond or the mouse no longer functions) or if a power outage occurs, contact a testing center administrator immediately. The administrator will restart the computer and return the exam to the point where the interruption occurred, with your score intact.

Certification benefits

At the conclusion of the exam, you will receive a score report, indicating whether you passed the exam. If your score meets or exceeds the passing standard (the minimum required score), you will be contacted by email by the Microsoft Certification Program team. The email message you receive will include your Microsoft Certification ID and links to online resources, including the Microsoft Certified Professional site. On this site, you can download or order a printed certificate, create a virtual business card, order an ID card, view and share your certification transcript, access the Logo Builder, and access other useful and interesting resources, including special offers from Microsoft and affiliated companies.

Depending on the level of certification you achieve, you will qualify to display one of three logos on your business card and other personal promotional materials. These logos attest to the fact that you are proficient in the applications or cross-application skills necessary to achieve the certification.

Microsoft
Office Specialist

Microsoft
Office Specialist Expert

Microsoft
Office Specialist Master

Using the Logo Builder, you can create a personalized certification logo that includes the MOS logo and the specific programs in which you have achieved certification. If you achieve MOS certification in multiple programs, you can include multiple certifications in one logo.

For more information

To learn more about the Microsoft Office Specialist exams and related courseware, visit:

http://www.microsoft.com/learning/en/us/mos-certification.aspx

Microsoft PowerPoint 2013

This book covers the skills you need to have for certification as a Microsoft Office Specialist in Microsoft PowerPoint 2013. Specifically, you need to be able to complete tasks that demonstrate the following skill sets:

1 Create and manage presentations

2 Insert and format slides and shapes

3 Create slide content

4 Apply transitions and animations

5 Manage multiple presentations

With these skills, you can create and manage the types of presentations that are most commonly used in a business environment.

Prerequisites

We assume that you have been working with PowerPoint 2013 for at least six months and that you know how to perform fundamental tasks that are not specifically mentioned in the objectives for this Microsoft Office Specialist exam. Before you begin studying for this exam, you might want to make sure you are familiar with the information in this section.

Understanding PowerPoint views

To help you create, organize, and display presentations, PowerPoint provides the following views:

- **Normal view** This is the default view. This view displays slide thumbnails in the Thumbnail pane and the active slide in the Slide pane. You can work with the content of a specific slide and enter development and delivery notes.

- **Outline view** This view displays slide titles and text content in the Outline pane, and the active slide in the Slide pane. You can modify text in the outline or on the adjacent slide. You can reorder slide content and slides in the outline.

- **Slide Sorter view** In this view, the slides of the presentation are displayed as thumbnails so that you can easily reorganize them and apply transitions and timings.

> **See Also** For information about slide transitions, see section 4.1, "Apply transitioning between slides" and section 4.3, "Set timing for transitions and animations." For information about slide timings, see section 1.5, "Configure and present slide shows."

- **Notes Page view** In this view, each slide is displayed at the top of a page where you can add speaker notes. In the Notes pane in Normal view, you can add speaker notes that consist of only text. However, to create speaker notes that contain elements other than text, such as a graphic or a chart, you must be in Notes Page view.

- **Reading view** In this view, each slide fills the screen. You use this view to preview the presentation. You cannot edit slides in this view.

- **Slide Show view** In this view, each slide fills the screen. You use this view to deliver the presentation to an audience.

- **Slide Master view, Handout Master view, or Notes Master view** In these views, you can make changes to the master slides that control the default design of the presentation components.

> **See Also** For more information about views, see section 1.3, "Customize presentation options and views."

Selecting text

Before you can edit or format existing text, you have to select it. You can select specific items as follows:

- **A word** Double-click it. The word and the space following it are selected. Punctuation following a word is not selected.

- **A bulleted list item** Click its bullet.

- **Adjacent words, lines, or paragraphs** Drag through them.

- **All the text in a placeholder** In the Slide pane, click inside the placeholder. Then press Ctrl+A or, on the Home tab, in the Editing group, click the Select button, and then click Select All.

- **All the text on a slide** In the Outline pane, click the slide icon.

- **All the objects on a slide** In the Slide pane, select any placeholder (so that it has a solid border). Then press Ctrl+A or, on the Home tab, in the Editing group, click the Select button, and then click Select All.

> **Tip** Clicking the Select button and then clicking Selection Pane displays the Selection pane, where you can specify whether each object on a slide should be displayed or hidden.

Selected text appears highlighted in the location where you made the selection—that is, either in the Slide pane in Normal view, or in the Outline pane in Outline view.

Saving presentations

You can save a presentation in multiple locations and in multiple formats. In the past, it was common to save files only locally on your computer. Now, many people save files to shared locations for the purpose of collaborating with other people or accessing the files from multiple computers and devices.

You can save a presentation to your local computer, to writable media, to a network location, or to an Internet location such as a Microsoft SharePoint site, corporate Microsoft SkyDrive Pro folder, personal SkyDrive folder, or another personal online storage folder.

The 2007 Microsoft Office system introduced a new set of file formats based on XML, called Microsoft Office Open XML Formats. By default, PowerPoint 2013 presentations are saved in the .pptx format, which is a PowerPoint-specific Open XML format. The .pptx format provides the following benefits:

- File sizes are smaller than with previous file formats.
- It is simpler to recover damaged content because XML files can be opened in a variety of text editors.
- Security is greater because .pptx files cannot contain macros, and personal data can easily be identified and removed from files.

Presentations saved in the .pptx format can be opened by PowerPoint 2013, PowerPoint 2010, and PowerPoint 2007. Users of earlier versions of PowerPoint can download a converter that they can use to open a .pptx file in their version of PowerPoint.

In addition to saving a presentation for use with PowerPoint 2013, you can save it in other formats, including the following:

- **PowerPoint Macro-Enabled Presentation (.pptm)** This format permits the storage of Microsoft Visual Basic for Applications (VBA) macro code in a presentation.
- **PowerPoint 97-2003 (.ppt)** This format removes formatting that would not be available to users of an earlier version of PowerPoint.

> **See Also** For information about maintaining backward compatibility, see section 1.4, "Configure presentations to print or save."

- **PowerPoint Template (.potx)** This format makes the presentation available as the starting point for other presentations. You can access templates that you save in the default location when you click the Custom heading on the New page of the Backstage view.

➤ **To display a list of all available file formats**

1. On the **Save As** page of the **Backstage** view, click the **Browse** button.
2. In the **Save As** dialog box, click the **Save as type** arrow to display the list.

➤ **To save a presentation in a specific format**

1. From the **Save As** page of the **Backstage** view, select the location in which you want to save the presentation.
2. In the **Save As** dialog box, enter a file name, select a file format, and then click **Save**.

1 Create and manage presentations

The skills tested in this section of the Microsoft Office Specialist exam for Microsoft PowerPoint 2013 relate to creating and managing presentations. Specifically, the following objectives are associated with this set of skills:

1.1 Create presentations

1.2 Format presentations by using slide masters

1.3 Customize presentation options and views

1.4 Configure presentations to print or save

1.5 Configure and present slide shows

As with other Office programs, you can create PowerPoint presentations from scratch or from a template. You can also create a presentation by importing a list of slide titles and content from another file. After creating a presentation, you can control its appearance not only by using themes and local formatting, but also by using slide masters, which are key to the efficient creation of consistently formatted presentations.

Traditionally, presentations are presented electronically. You can configure a presentation for someone else to play either locally or online, or you can configure it for you to present in person. You can also print presentations and various aspects thereof, either to provide all the information that is in the presentation, or to provide a convenient surface for audience members to follow along and take notes.

This chapter guides you in studying ways of creating presentations, applying themes, creating and modifying slide masters, and configuring properties, options, and slide shows.

> **Practice Files** To complete the practice tasks in this chapter, you need the practice files contained in the MOSPowerPoint2013\Objective1 practice file folder. For more information, see "Download the practice files" in this book's Introduction.

1.1 Create presentations

When creating a PowerPoint presentation, you have several options, including the following:

- Create a blank presentation that consists only of a title slide, add slides and slide content, and then format the presentation.

- Import a list of slide titles from a text document, add slide content and a title slide, and then format the presentation.

- Import slide titles and content from a Microsoft Word file, add a title slide, and then format the presentation.

- Create a preformatted or prepopulated presentation based on a local or online template.

When PowerPoint is running, you can create a blank or prepopulated presentation from the New page of the Backstage view.

By default, a new presentation includes only a title slide. You can add blank content slides to the presentation, or copy or move slides from another presentation.

To create an unformatted presentation that includes slides, you can import a text file or Word document that contains the slide information. PowerPoint creates unformatted Title And Content slides corresponding to the slide titles specified in the source file. When creating a presentation from text file content, you can create only slide titles, because text files don't support formatting options that would inform PowerPoint of how you want to use the content. When creating a presentation from Word file content, however, you can format the content by applying multiple heading levels.

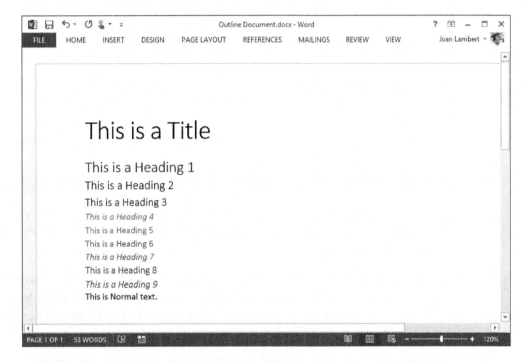

PowerPoint creates slides, slide titles, and multiple levels of bulleted content based on the heading levels assigned within the Word document. PowerPoint uses only the headings and not other document content. Paragraphs styled as Title or Heading1 become slide titles, and paragraphs styled as Heading2 through Heading9 become bullet points.

If you save an outline containing styled headings as a Word document (.doc or .docx) or a Rich Text Format (RTF) file (.rtf), you can create a new presentation by opening the outline from PowerPoint, or add the outline slides to the existing presentation by importing the outline.

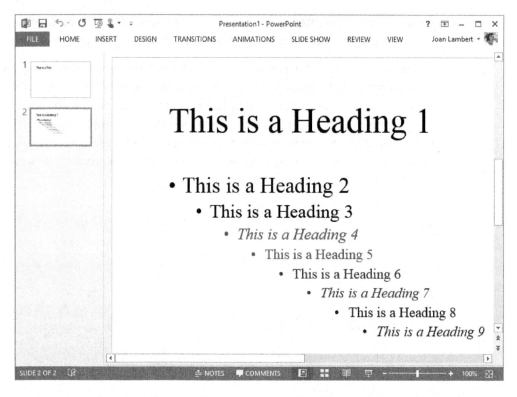

Creating attractive presentations from scratch can be time-consuming. You can save time by basing your presentation on one of the templates that come with PowerPoint. Two types of templates are available when creating a new presentation:

- **Design template** This is a blank presentation with a theme, and sometimes graphics, already applied to it. Some templates supply only a title slide and leave it to you to add the other slides you need; other templates supply an example of each of the available slide layouts.

- **Content template** From the PowerPoint starting screen, you can preview and download presentation templates that are available from the Office website. These templates provide not only the design but also suggestions for content that is appropriate for different types of presentations, such as reports or product launches. After downloading the template, you simply customize the content provided in the template to meet your needs.

➤ **To create a blank presentation**

→ Start PowerPoint. On the start screen, press **Esc** or click **Blank Presentation**.

→ On the **New** page of the **Backstage** view, click **Blank Presentation**.

→ From the program window, press **Ctrl+N**.

➤ **To create a presentation based on a template**

→ On the start screen or on the **New** page of the **Backstage** view, do one of the following:

○ Click a featured template. If color options are shown in the preview window, click the color scheme you want, and then click **Create**.

○ Double-click a featured template to create a presentation with the default color scheme.

○ Enter a template type or subject in the **Search** box, and then press **Enter** or click the **Search** button. Click a template thumbnail to preview its contents, and then create a presentation by clicking **Create** in the preview window; or double-click the template thumbnail to create a presentation without first previewing it.

○ Click the **Personal** heading, and then double-click a custom or downloaded workbook template.

➤ **To create a presentation based on a text file**

1. Create a text file that contains the slide titles for the slides you want.

2. Start PowerPoint. From the **Open** page of the **Backstage** view, browse to the folder that contains the text file.

3. In the **Open** dialog box, in the **File Type** list, click **All Files** or **All Outlines**.

4. Double-click the text file to import it into PowerPoint, and then create blank slides corresponding to the slide titles in the file.

➤ **To create a presentation based on a Word outline**

1. Create a Word document that contains the slide titles and bulleted list content for the slides you want.

2. In the Word document, apply the Title or Heading1 style to text that equates to new slide titles, the Heading2 style to text that equates to first-level bullet points on the slide, and the Heading3 style to text that equates to second-level bullet points. Then save the file.

3. To create a presentation based on the outline, start PowerPoint, and then do the following:

   a. From the **Open** page of the **Backstage** view, browse to the folder that contains the Word document.

   b. In the **Open** dialog box, in the **File Type** list, click **All Files** or **All Outlines**.

   c. Double-click the Word document to create a presentation populated with slides corresponding to the slide titles in the document.

Or

To insert slides based on the outline into an existing presentation, open the presentation, and then do the following:

   a. In the **Slides** pane, click to position the insertion bar in the location where you want to insert the new slides.

   b. On the **Insert** tab, in the **Slides** group, click the **New Slide** arrow, and then click **Slides from Outline**.

   c. In the **Insert Outline** dialog box, browse to the folder that contains the Word document, and then double-click the Word document to insert slides corresponding to the slide titles in the document.

Practice tasks

The practice files for these tasks are located in the MOSPowerPoint2013\Objective1 practice file folder. Save the results of the tasks in the same folder.

- Start PowerPoint and create a blank presentation.

- Create a photo album based on a presentation template that you like in the Photo Album category.

- From within PowerPoint, open the *PowerPoint_1-1a* text file to create a presentation based on the file contents. Save the presentation as *MyTextPresentation.pptx*.

- From within PowerPoint, open the *PowerPoint_1-1b* document to create a presentation based on the file contents. Save the presentation as *MyDocPresentation.pptx*.

1.2 Format presentations by using slide masters

PowerPoint uses two types of elements to control the appearance of slides:

- **Themes** These control the colors, fonts, effects, and background style of all the slides in a presentation. Many themes include color variants that are identical in all ways other than the color scheme.

- **Slide masters** These control the layout, master style, and static slide elements of specific types of slides.

These elements are closely interrelated in that applying a theme also applies a slide master, and applying a slide master also applies a theme.

Apply and modify presentation themes

By default, PowerPoint applies the Office theme to all new, blank presentations. To quickly change the appearance of a presentation, you can apply a different theme. To change the appearance of all new presentations, you can set a different theme as the default.

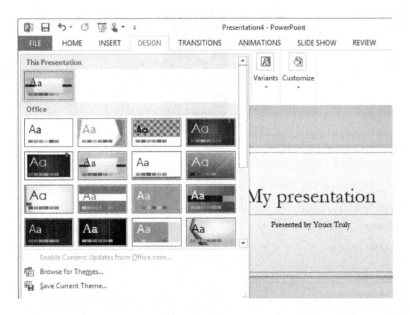

After selecting a theme, you can select a variant, which is simply the same theme with a different color scheme.

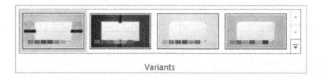

Variants

If you like some components of the theme but not others, you can change the following:

- **Colors** Every presentation, even a blank one, has an associated set of 12 comple-
  mentary colors: four Text/Background colors for dark or light text on a dark or light
  background; Accent 1 through Accent 6 for the colors of objects other than text;
  Hyperlink to draw attention to hyperlinks; and Followed Hyperlink to indicate visited
  hyperlinks. Of these colors, 10 appear with light to dark gradients in the various
  color palettes. (The two background colors are not represented in these palettes.)

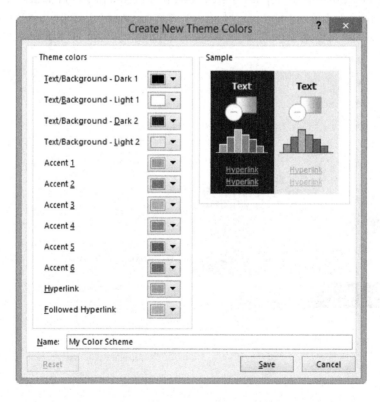

- **Fonts** Every presentation, even a blank one, has an associated set of two fonts. The Office section of the Fonts gallery lists the 25 built-in combinations of heading and body fonts. The top font in each combination is used for titles and headings, and the bottom font is used for regular text.

> **Tip** If none of the color schemes is exactly what you are looking for, you can create your own. For example, you might create a custom color scheme that incorporates your organization's corporate colors. If none of the preconfigured font sets is appropriate for your purposes, you can create a custom font set. Custom color schemes and font sets are saved in your \AppData\Roaming\Microsoft\Templates\Document Themes\Theme Fonts folder and are available to all Office 2013 programs.

- **Effects** The Effects gallery displays the 15 built-in effect styles that you can associate with a theme. If one of the effect styles is applied to the current presentation, a box surrounds that effect.

- **Background style** The Background Styles gallery displays three subtly patterned variations of each of four background colors that you can assign to the theme.

Changes made to a component of a theme are stored with the presentation and do not affect the default theme. If you modify the color scheme, font set, effects, or background associated with the theme and want to use the modified combination again, you can save it as a custom theme in your Document Themes folder, and it will become available from the Themes gallery.

➤ **To apply a theme**

→ On the **Design** tab, in the **Themes** gallery, click the theme you want.

> **Tip** If the thumbnail of the theme you want is visible, you can click it without displaying the entire gallery. You can also scroll through the gallery to show one row of thumbnails at a time.

→ If the theme is stored outside of the default Document Themes folder, click **Browse for Themes** on the **Themes** menu, browse to the theme you want, and then click **Open**.

➤ **To modify a theme**

→ On the **Design** tab, in the **Variants** gallery, click the variant you want.

→ On the **Design** tab, on the **Variants** menu, click **Colors**, **Fonts**, **Effects**, or **Background Styles**, and then in the corresponding gallery, click the formatting option you want.

➤ **To create a custom color scheme**

1. Apply the color scheme that is closest to the one you want.

2. On the **Design** tab, in the **Variants** group, click the **More** button. On the **Variants** menu, click **Colors**, and then click **Customize Colors**.

3. In the **Create New Theme Colors** dialog box, click the box to the right of the presentation element you want to change.

4. On the menu that appears, do one of the following:

   ○ In the **Theme Colors** or **Standard Colors** palette, click the color you want to apply to the selected element.

   > **Tip** Choosing a color from the Theme Colors palette ensures that the colors within the presentation remain coordinated, even when you apply a different them to the presentation.

   ○ Click **More Colors**. On either the **Standard** page or the **Custom** page of the **Colors** dialog box, click the color you want, and then click **OK**.

5. In the **Name** box at the bottom of the **Create New Theme Colors** dialog box, assign a name to the new color scheme, and then click **Save**.

➤ **To create a custom font set**

1. On the **Design** tab, in the **Variants** group, click the **More** button. On the **Variants** menu, click **Fonts**, and then click **Customize Fonts**.

2. In the **Create New Theme Fonts** dialog box, select the heading font and body font you want to use.

3. In the **Name** box, assign a name to the new color scheme, and then click **Save**.

➤ **To save a custom theme**

1. Modify the colors, fonts, effects, and background of the current theme to suit your needs.

2. On the **Design** tab, on the **Themes** menu, click **Save Current Theme**.

3. In the **Save Current Theme** dialog box, enter a name for the theme, and then click **Save**.

Apply and modify slide masters

When you create a new presentation, its slides assume the formatting of the presentation's slide master, which by default contains placeholders for a title, the date, the slide number, and footer information. These placeholders control the position of the corresponding elements on the slide.

Each slide master includes multiple slide templates, called *layouts*, that control the layout of content on specific types of slides. Typical slide layouts are Title, Title And Content, Two Content, Section Header, and Blank. Other layouts are specific to the type of content associated with the slide master; for example, the slide master for a photo album might include layouts for Album Cover, Portrait With Caption, or Panorama With Caption.

When working in a presentation, you can make changes to the design elements provided by the slide master, but you can change the default settings only on the slide master and layouts. When you change a design element on the slide master, all the slide layouts and slides reflect the change.

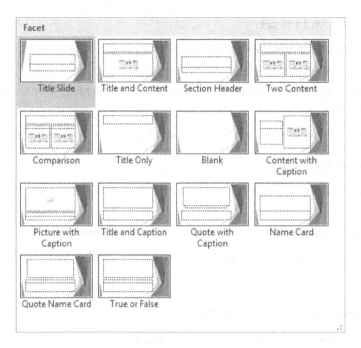

You can modify all the slides in a presentation by modifying the slide master on which all layouts are based, or you can modify one type of slide by modifying the layout applied to that slide. If you modify formatting directly on a slide, or insert a slide from another source and want to match it to those in your presentation, you can apply or reset the slide layout to revert its formatting to the default.

To make changes to a presentation's master, you switch to Slide Master view, which adds a Slide Master tab to the ribbon and hides the tabs that aren't needed. In this view, the slide master thumbnail is displayed at the top of the Overview pane, followed by thumbnails of its associated layouts.

From the Slide Master tab, you can modify elements of the slide master in the following ways:

- Apply a theme or modify the colors, fonts, or effects associated with the current theme.

- Control the background color, texture, and graphics.

- Specify which placeholders appear on all slides.

- Add custom elements that you want to appear on all slides, including headers, footers, slide numbers, and graphics such as logos.

The changes to the slide master are automatically applied to all the layouts.

> **Tip** While working in Slide Master view, you can format text placeholders, insert graphic objects, and add animations and transitions by using the same techniques you would use to perform those tasks with slides.

➤ **To apply a slide layout**

1. To apply the layout to only one slide, display the slide in **Normal** view or select it in **Slide Sorter** view.

   Or

   To apply the layout to multiple slides, display the presentation in **Slide Sorter** view, and then select the slides you want to modify.

2. On the **Home** tab, in the **Slides** group, click the **Layout** button, and then click the layout you want to apply.

➤ **To reset slide content to the layout defaults**

→ Select the slide or slides you want to reset. Then on the **Home** tab, in the **Slides** group, click the **Reset** button.

➤ **To switch to Slide Master view**

→ On the **View** tab, in the **Master Views** group, click the **Slide Master** button.

➤ **To close Slide Master view**

→ On the **Slide Master** tab, in the **Close** group, click the **Close Master View** button.

→ On the **View Shortcuts** toolbar at the right end of the status bar, click any view button.

➤ **To modify a slide master**

1. In the **Navigation** pane, click the slide master to select it.

2. To specify the slide elements that are controlled by the slide master, follow these steps:

   a. On the **Slide Master** tab, in the **Master Layout** group, click the **Master Layout** button.

   b. In the **Master Layout** dialog box, select the check boxes of the elements you want the slide master to control. Options include **Title**, **Text**, **Date**, **Slide number**, and **Footer**. Then click **OK**.

3. To insert an image on all slide layouts, follow these steps:

   a. On the **Insert** tab, in the **Images** group, click **Pictures**.

   b. In the **Insert Picture** dialog box, browse to the folder containing the picture you want to insert, click the picture, and then click **Insert**.

   c. On the slide master, move, size, and format the picture as you want it to appear on all slide layouts.

➤ **To insert content placeholders on a slide layout**

1. In the **Master Layout** group, click the **Insert Placeholder** arrow, and then click **Content**, **Text**, **Picture**, **Chart**, **Table**, **SmartArt**, **Media**, or **Online Image**.

2. Click on the slide to insert a placeholder of the default size and shape, or drag to draw a placeholder.

3. Change the size, location, outline, or fill of the placeholder by using the tools on the **Format** tool tab.

➤ **To modify placeholders on a slide master or layout**

➜ Click a placeholder, and then change its size, location, outline, or fill by using the tools on the **Format** tool tab.

➤ **To modify text on a slide master or layout**

➜ Select static text or placeholder text, and then use the commands on the **Home** tab to modify the paragraph or font settings.

➤ **To configure the background image on a slide master or layout**

➜ On the **Slide Master** tab, in the **Background** group, click the **Background Styles** button, and then click the background you want to apply to all slide layouts.

➜ In the **Background** group, click the **Background Styles** button, and then click **Format Background**. In the **Format Background** pane, configure the fill style, color, and transparency.

➜ To modify the background of the selected slide layout and all other slide layouts, configure the settings in the **Format Background** pane, and then click **Apply to All**.

➜ To remove the slide master background from a selected slide layout, in the **Background** group, select the **Hide Background Graphics** check box.

➤ **To control header and footer elements on a slide master or layout**

1. On the **Insert** tab, in the **Text** group, click the **Header & Footer** button.

2. In the **Header and Footer** dialog box, select the check boxes for the elements you want to display. Options include **Date and time**, **Slide number**, and **Footer**.

3. If you select the **Date and time** check box, select the **Update automatically** option, and then select the date and time format you want from the list.

Or

Select the **Fixed** option, and then enter the date and time you want to display.

4. To suppress the header and footer elements on the Title Slide layout, select the **Don't show on title slide** check box.

5. In the **Header and Footer** dialog box, select the check boxes for the elements you want to display. Options include **Date and time**, **Slide number**, and **Footer**.

➤ **To modify a slide layout independent of the slide master**

→ On the **Slide Master** tab, in the **Master Layout** group, select or clear the **Title** and **Footers** check boxes to specify whether the slide master sets these elements for the slide master.

→ In the **Master Layout** group, from the **Insert Placeholder** list, insert the elements for which you want to configure space on the slide layout.

➤ **To add a layout to a slide master**

→ On the **Slide Master** tab, in the **Edit Master** group, click **Insert Layout**.

➤ **To remove one or more layouts from a slide master**

→ In the **Slides** pane, select the slide layout or layouts you want to remove. Then press the **Delete** key or on the **Slide Master** tab, in the **Edit Master** group, click the **Delete** button.

> **Tip** Only slide layouts that are not currently in use can be deleted. Pointing to a slide layout displays, in a ScreenTip, a list of slides to which the layout is applied.

Practice tasks

The practice files for these tasks are located in the MOSPowerPoint2013\Objective1 practice file folder. Save the results of the tasks in the same folder.

- Open the *PowerPoint_1-2a* presentation, and complete the following tasks:
  - ○ Apply the Vapor theme to the presentation.
  - ○ Modify the theme by applying one of the two theme variants that has a white background.
  - ○ Modify the theme by applying the Calibri font set.
  - ○ Save the modified theme in the default location as *MyMOSTheme.thmx*.
  - ○ Save the modified presentation as *MySales.pptx*.
- Open the *PowerPoint_1-2b* presentation, and complete the following tasks:
  - ○ Display Slide Master view. Apply the Ion Boardroom theme to the slide master.
  - ○ Insert the *PowerPoint_1-2c* image on the slide master. Position the image so that it aligns with the right margin of the slide master and the horizontal centerline of the content pane. Then scroll through the Slides pane and notice which layouts the image appears on.
- Delete the Name Card, Title And Vertical Text, and Vertical Title And Text slide layouts from the slide master.
- Close Slide Master view, and then complete the following tasks:
  - ○ Apply the Title Slide layout to slide 1.
  - ○ Insert a Quote With Caption slide after slide 1. Enter the text *What will you do this summer?* between the quotation marks, center the text in the text box, and then set the font size to 80 points.
  - ○ Apply the Comparison slide layout to slide 3. Move the original text from the left column heading placeholder to the left column, and move the final bullet from the left column to the right column. Then enter *Positive* as the left column heading and *Negative* as the right column heading.
  - ○ Apply the Title And Content slide layout to slides 4 and 5.
  - ○ Save the modified presentation as *MyVacation.pptx*.

1.3 Customize presentation options and views

Manage presentation properties

In PowerPoint 2013, the properties of a presentation are easily accessible from the Info page of the Backstage view. You can view and modify some properties directly on the Info page, or you can work in the Document Panel or Properties dialog box.

Properties ˅

Size	112KB
Slides	31
Hidden slides	0
Words	604
Notes	0
Title	Sample Presentation
Tags	Add a tag
Comments	Add comments
Multimedia clips	0
Presentation format	Custom
Template	ITA-Theme-Dark
Status	Add text
Categories	Office 2013;Microsoft
Subject	MOS certification
Hyperlink Base	Add text
Company	OTSI
Stage	Final

➤ **To set or change basic optional properties**

→ On the **Info** page of the **Backstage** view, click the property to activate it, and then add or change information.

➤ **To display the Document Panel**

→ On the **Info** page of the **Backstage** view, click **Properties**, and then click **Show Document Panel**.

➤ **To display the Properties dialog box**

→ On the **Info** page of the **Backstage** view, click **Properties**, and then click **Advanced Properties**. Editable properties are located on the **Summary** and **Custom** pages of this **Properties** dialog box.

→ In File Explorer, right-click the file, and then click **Properties**. Editable properties are located on the **Details** page of this **Properties** dialog box.

> **Tip** In Windows 8, File Explorer has replaced Windows Explorer. Throughout this book, we refer to this utility by its Windows 8 name. If your computer is running Windows 7 or an earlier version of Windows, use Windows Explorer instead.

Configure slide setup options

By default, PowerPoint 2013 slides are sized for a widescreen display (13.333 inches by 7.5 inches). The slides are oriented horizontally, with slide numbers starting at 1. You can set the size and orientation of the slides, and the orientation of notes, handouts, and outlines, to fit your intended distribution methods.

In the Slide Size dialog box, you can select from the following slide sizes:

- **On-screen Show** For an electronic slide show on screens of various aspects (4:3, 16:9, or 16:10)

- **Letter Paper** For a presentation printed on 8.5-by-11-inch US letter-size paper

- **Ledger Paper** For a presentation printed on 11-by-17-inch ledger-size paper

- **A3 Paper, A4 Paper, B4 (ISO) Paper, B5 (ISO) Paper** For a presentation printed on paper of various standard international sizes

- **35mm Slides** For 35mm slides to be used in a carousel with a projector

- **Overhead** For transparencies for an overhead projector

- **Banner** For a webpage banner

- **Widescreen** For a widescreen monitor display

- **Custom** For slides that are a nonstandard size

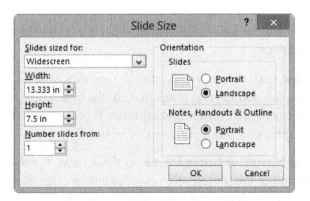

➤ **To set the size of slides**

1. On the **Design** tab, in the **Customize** group, click the **Slide Size** button, and then click **Custom Slide Size**.

2. In the **Slide Size** dialog box, do either of the following, and then click **OK**:

   ○ In the **Slides sized for** list, select the size you want.

   ○ In the **Slides sized for** list, click **Custom**. Then in the **Width** and **Height** boxes, specify the slide dimensions you want.

3. In the **Microsoft PowerPoint** dialog box that opens, click **Maximize** to ensure that no blank space is added to the slide, or **Ensure Fit** to ensure that all existing content fits on the slide.

➤ **To set the orientation of slides, notes, handouts, or the outline**

1. On the **Design** tab, in the **Customize** group, click the **Slide Size** button, and then click **Custom Slide Size**.

2. In the **Orientation** area of the **Slide Size** dialog box, select the **Portrait** or **Landscape** option for **Slides** and for **Notes, Handouts & Outline**, and then click **OK**.

Display different views of a presentation

PowerPoint has several views in which you can create, organize, and display slides:

- **Normal** This is the default view. You can work with the content of a specific slide and enter development and delivery notes.

- **Slide Sorter** In this view, the slides of the presentation are displayed as thumbnails so that you can easily reorganize them and apply transitions and timings.

- **Reading View** In this view, each slide fills the screen. You use this view to preview the presentation.

- **Slide Show** In this view, each slide fills the screen. You use this view to deliver the presentation to an audience.

- **Notes Page** In this view, each slide is displayed at the top of a page where you can add speaker notes. You can add speaker notes that consist of only text in the Notes pane in Normal view. However, to create speaker notes that contain elements other than text, such as a graphic or a chart, you must be in Notes Page view.

- **Slide Master, Handout Master, or Notes Master** In these views, the masters that control the default design of the presentation components are displayed. You can make changes to the overall design by working with these masters.

> **Tip** While developing a presentation, you can display it in grayscale to preview the color scheme as it will appear when printed on a monochrome printer.

➤ **To display a different view of a presentation**

→ On the **View** tab, in the **Presentation Views** group, click the **Normal**, **Outline View**, **Slide Sorter**, **Notes Page**, or **Reading View** button.

→ On the **View Shortcuts** toolbar at the right end of the status bar, click the **Normal**, **Slide Sorter**, or **Reading View** button.

➤ **To display a presentation in grayscale**

→ On the **View** tab, in the **Color/Grayscale** group, click the **Grayscale** button.

Practice tasks

The practice file for these tasks is located in the MOSPowerPoint2013\Objective1 practice file folder. Save the results of the tasks in the same folder.

- Open the *PowerPoint_1-3* presentation, and then complete the following tasks:
  - ○ Set the title of the presentation to *Vacation Ideas* and the Status to *In Progress*.
  - ○ Display the presentation in Slide Sorter view, and then select all the slides.
  - ○ Set the slide size to On-screen Show (4:3), and then click the Maximize option. Notice the effect of this selection on the text on slide 2 and the image on slides 3 through 5.
  - ○ Undo the slide size change. Then reselect the slide size, and click the Ensure Fit option.
  - ○ Display the presentation in Slide Master view. Select the image on the slide master, and then invoke the Reset Picture & Size command in the Adjust group on the Format tool tab. Ensure that the image is center-aligned with the content pane, and then close Slide Master view.
  - ○ Display the presentation as it would appear in grayscale, and then as it would appear in black and white. Notice the changes required to make the presentation content visible and effective in each of those color schemes.

1.4 Configure presentations to print or save

Print presentations

A PowerPoint presentation can include many types of information; the information on the slides is intended for the audience, and the information stored in the slide notes is usually intended for the presenter.

> **Tip** If you use speaker notes when delivering a presentation to an audience, you can enter text in the Notes pane in Normal view. If you want speaker notes that include pictures or other supporting materials in addition to text, you can develop the speaker notes in Notes Page view.

You can print various forms of the presentation for different purposes. You can select from standard print layout options for slides, notes pages, outlines, and handouts.

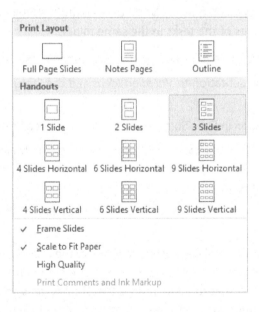

When you are ready to print, you can adjust any of the following settings:

- **Specify the printer to use** You can specify the printer you want to use and set its properties (such as paper source and image compression).

- **Specify which slides to print** You can print all the slides, the selected slides, or the current slide. You can print only specific slides by clicking the Slides box and entering slide numbers and ranges separated by commas (no spaces). For example, enter *1,5,10-12* to print slides 1, 5, 10, 11, and 12.

- **Print hidden slides** You can include slides in the printed version that will be hidden in the electronic presentation.

- **Specify what to print** You can print slides (one per page), notes pages (one half-size slide per page with space for notes), an outline, or handouts. When printing handouts, you can specify the number of slides that print on each page (1, 2, 3, 4, 6, or 9) and the order in which the slides appear on the page.

- **Put a frame around slides** You can print a frame around the slides on the printed page.

- **Scale slides to fit the paper** If you haven't set the size of the slides to match the size of the paper in the printer, PowerPoint can automatically reduce or increase the size of the slides to fit the paper when you print them.

- **Print in high quality** For final output, you can specify that the slides be printed in the printer's highest quality.

- **Print comments and ink markup** You can print electronic or handwritten notes attached to the presentation so that you can review them along with the slides.

- **Print and collate multiple copies** If you want to print multiple copies of a presentation, you can specify whether complete copies should be printed one at a time.

- **Specify the color range** You can print your presentation in color (color on a color printer and grayscale on a monochrome printer), grayscale (on a color or monochrome printer), or pure black and white (no gray on either a color or monochrome printer).

> **Tip** Most presentations are created in color. If you have a color printer, you can specify whether to print the presentation in color or in grayscale.

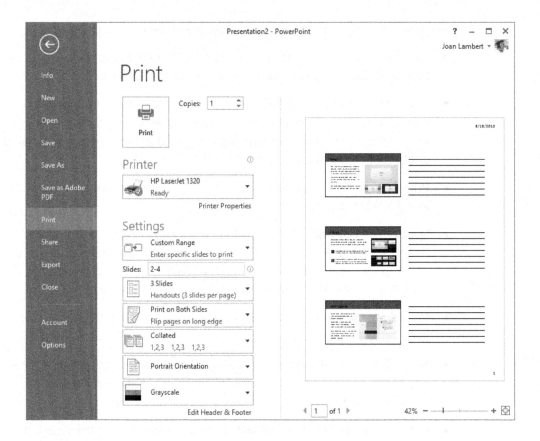

> ### To print selections from presentations

> → On the **Print** page of the **Backstage** view, in the first list in the **Settings** area, click **Print All Slides**, **Print Selection**, or **Print Current Slide**; or click **Custom Range** and then, in the **Slides** box, enter the slides you want to print.

> → On the **Print** page of the **Backstage** view, in the **Slides** box, enter the slides you want to print.

> ### To print speaker notes

> → On the **Print** page of the **Backstage** view, in the second list in the **Settings** area, in the **Print Layout** gallery, click **Notes Pages**. Configure any additional print settings, and then click **Print**.

> ### To print an outline

> → In the second list in the **Settings** area, in the **Print Layout** gallery, click **Outline**. Configure any additional print settings, and then click **Print**.

➤ **To print handouts**

→ In the second list in the **Settings** area, in the **Handouts** gallery, click the handout configuration you want. Configure any additional print settings, and then click **Print**.

➤ **To configure print colors for a presentation**

→ On the **Print** page of the **Backstage** view, in the final list in the **Settings** area, click **Color**, **Grayscale**, or **Pure Black and White**.

Prepare presentations for distribution

If you work with people who are using a version of PowerPoint earlier than 2007, they can install the free Microsoft Office Compatibility Pack For Word, Excel, And PowerPoint File Formats from the Microsoft Download Center at *download.microsoft.com*. The Compatibility Pack doesn't provide additional functionality, but it does enable users to open .pptx files in the earlier version of PowerPoint.

If you want to ensure that all the elements of a presentation will be available to users of an earlier version of PowerPoint, you can save it in the PowerPoint 97-2003 Presentation file format. Before saving a presentation in this format, you can use the Compatibility Checker to identify any presentation content that is not supported in previous versions of PowerPoint. You can then decide how to handle any reported issues.

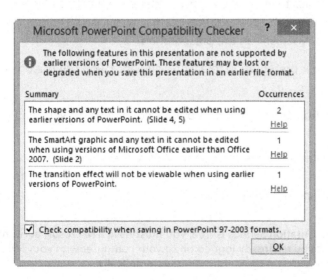

If you intend to run your presentation on a computer other than the one on which you developed it, you need to ensure that the fonts, linked objects, and any other necessary items are available to the presentation. You can use the Package For CD feature to save all presentation components to a CD (not a DVD) or other type of removable media. You can include more than one presentation, and you can specify the order in which the presentations should run. As part of the packaging process, you can assign a password and remove extraneous information from the packaged file.

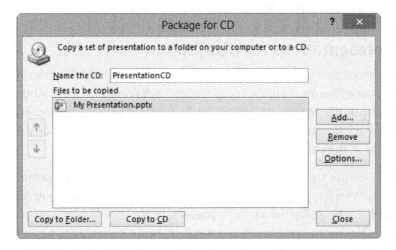

After PowerPoint assembles the files, it creates a folder of supporting files and adds an autorun file. When you insert the presentation CD into your CD/DVD drive, the AutoPlay dialog box opens so that you can run the presentation.

If you want to deliver your presentation to a wider audience, you can use one of the following methods:

- Save the presentation as a video that is optimized for web delivery, and post the video online.

- Deliver the presentation online through the Office Presentation Service. You can use this free service to share a presentation live and make it available for download during or after the presentation.

> **Tip** The Office Presentation Service is free; you must have a Microsoft account to connect to it, but if you're already logged on to your computer with your Microsoft account, the service picks up that information automatically.

➤ **To check for features that are not supported in previous versions of PowerPoint**

1. On the **Info** page of the **Backstage** view, click **Check for Issues**, and then click **Check Compatibility**.

2. Make a note of any issues reported in the **Compatibility Checker** dialog box, and then click **OK**.

➤ **To maintain backward compatibility with previous versions of PowerPoint**

1. When saving the presentation, choose the previous file format in the **Save as type** list.

2. If prompted to do so, click **Continue** in the **Microsoft Word Compatibility Checker** window to convert unsupported features.

➤ **To package a presentation for delivery on another computer**

1. On the **Export** page of the **Backstage** view, click **Package Presentation for CD**, and then click **Package for CD**.

2. In the **Package for CD** dialog box, provide a disc name in the **Name the CD** box, and then click **Options**.

> **Tip** The disc name is shown as the drive name in File Explorer when the disc is in the disc drive.

3. In the **Options** dialog box, do any of the following, and then click **OK**:

  ○ Select or clear the **Linked files** and **Embedded TrueType fonts** check boxes to specify which elements to package with the presentation.

  ○ Set passwords to open or modify the presentation.

  ○ If you want to run the Document Inspector before packaging the presentation, select the **Inspect presentations for inappropriate or private information** check box.

4. Do one of the following:

  ○ Insert a blank CD in your CD/DVD burner, and if the **AutoPlay** dialog box opens, close it. Then in the **Package for CD** dialog box, click **Copy to CD**.

  ○ In the **Package for CD** dialog box, click **Copy to Folder**. In the **Copy to Folder** dialog box, specify the folder in which you want to store the package, and then click **OK**.

5. If you selected the **Linked files** check box in step 3, click **Yes** in the Microsoft PowerPoint dialog box to verify that you trust the source of the linked content.

6. If you selected the **Inspect presentations...** check box in step 3, follow the steps in the Document Inspector, and then click **Close**.

7. When a message box indicates that the packaging operation was successful, click **No** to indicate that you don't want to copy the same package again, and then click **Close**.

➤ **To package a presentation as a video**

1. On the **Export** page of the **Backstage** view, click **Create a Video**.

2. On the **Create a Video** page, click **Internet & DVD** in the first list.

3. If you have recorded timings or narration with the presentation, select either **Use Recorded Timings and Narrations** or **Don't Use Recorded Timings and Narrations** in the second list, to indicate whether to package those elements with the video.

> **Tip** If you want to record the timings and narration now, you can start that process from the second list or from the Slide Show tab.

4. If you selected the **Don't Use...** option in step 3, in the **Seconds spent on each slide** box, enter the time to display each slide.

5. On the **Create a Video** page, click the **Create Video** button.

6. In the **Save As** dialog box, do the following, and then click **Save**:

    a. Browse to the folder in which you want to save the video.

    b. Enter a name for the video in the **File name** box.

    c. Click **MPEG-4 Video** or **Windows Media Video** in the **Save as type** list.

➤ **To share a presentation through the Office Presentation Service**

1. On the **Share** page of the **Backstage** view, click **Present Online**.

2. In the **Present Online** pane, if a list at the top contains multiple online presentation options, click **Office Presentation Service** in the list.

3. If you want to make the presentation available for download, select the **Enable remote viewers to download the presentation** check box.

4. Click the **Present Online** button.

5. After the service connects by using your Microsoft account, click **Copy Link** or **Send in Email**, and provide the presentation link to your intended viewers. Then click **Start Presentation**.

Practice tasks

The practice files for these tasks are located in the MOSPowerPoint2013\Objective1 practice file folder. Save the results of the tasks in the same folder.

- Open the *PowerPoint_1-4a* presentation, and complete the following tasks:
  - ○ Print one set of handouts with three slides per page in color.
  - ○ Print a set of speaker's notes in grayscale.
- Open the *PowerPoint_1-4b* presentation, and complete the following tasks:
  - ○ Check the presentation for compatibility with PowerPoint 2003.
  - ○ Save the presentation as *My2003Show* in a format that allows it to be opened and edited in that program.

1.5 Configure and present slide shows

Configure custom slide shows

If you need to deliver variations of a presentation to different audiences, you can maintain one presentation containing all the slides you are likely to need for all the audiences. Then you can select the slides that are appropriate for a specific audience and assign them to a custom slide show.

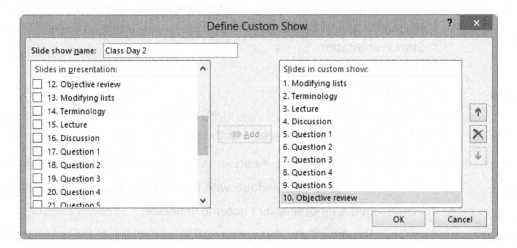

When you need to deliver the custom version of the presentation, you open the main presentation and display only the subset of slides by choosing the custom slide show from a list.

When you are preparing to deliver a slide show, you can configure the slide show settings to reflect the environment in which it will be presented. In the Set Up Show dialog box, you can specify the following:

- How the presentation will be delivered
- Whether all slides will be shown, or only a subset of the available slides
- Whether an automatic slide show will loop continuously, be shown without narration, and be shown without animation
- Whether slide timings will be used
- Whether your hardware setup includes multiple monitors and, if so, whether you want to use Presenter view
- What pen color and laser pointer color should be used

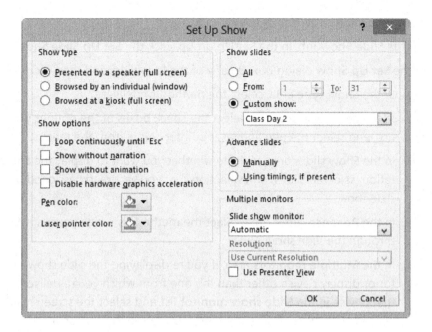

> **To create a custom slide show**

1. On the **Slide Show** tab, in the **Start Slide Show** group, click the **Custom Slide Show** button, and then click **Custom Shows**.

2. In the **Custom Shows** dialog box, click **New**.

> **Tip** To create a custom slide show that is similar to an existing custom slide show, click the slide show, click Copy, and then edit the copy.

3. In the **Define Custom Show** dialog box, enter a name for the custom show in the **Slide show name** box.

4. In the **Slides in presentation** list, select the check boxes of the slides you want to include in the custom slide show, and then click **Add**.

5. In the **Slides in custom show** list, select any slide you want to reorder, and then click the arrows to reorder the slides.

6. In the **Define Custom Show** dialog box, click **OK**.

7. In the **Custom Shows** dialog box, click **Close** to return to the presentation or click **Show** to run the custom slide show.

➤ **To set up a slide show for delivery**

1. On the **Slide Show** tab, in the **Set Up** group, click the **Set Up Slide Show** button.

2. In the **Set Up Show** dialog box, do any of the following, and then click **OK**:

   ○ In the **Show type** area, select the method of delivery.

   ○ In the **Show options** area, select the check boxes of the options you want to use, and select the pen and laser pointer colors from the menus.

   ○ In the **Show slides** area, indicate whether you want to display the entire presentation, selected slides, or a selection that you've already assigned to a custom slide show.

   ○ In the **Advance slides** area, select the method by which you want to move through the slide show.

   ○ In the **Multiple monitors** area, if you're displaying the slide show on a monitor or display device other than the one from which you're delivering it, select that device in the **Slide show monitor** list and select the screen resolution at which you want to display the slide show in the **Resolution** list. If you want to display the presenter notes on one monitor and the slide show on the other, select the **Use Presenter View** check box.

➤ **To run a custom slide show**

→ On the **Slide Show** tab, in the **Start Slide Show** group, click the **Custom Slide Show** button, and then click the custom slide show you want to run.

   Or

1. In **Slide Show** view, move the mouse to display the navigation toolbar in the lower-left corner.

2. On the navigation toolbar, click the **Navigation** button (labeled with an ellipsis), click **Custom Show**, and then click the show you want.

Present slide shows

When delivering a presentation, you can move from slide to slide in the following ways:

- **Manually** You control when you move by clicking the mouse button, pressing keys, or clicking commands.

- **Automatically** PowerPoint displays each slide for a predefined length of time and then displays the next slide.

For automatic slide shows, the length of time a slide appears on the screen is controlled by the slide timing that you configure. You can apply timings to a single slide, to a group of slides, or to an entire presentation, either by allocating time to each slide or by rehearsing the presentation while PowerPoint automatically tracks and sets the timings for you.

Display time for the current slide

Display time recorded for the presentation so far

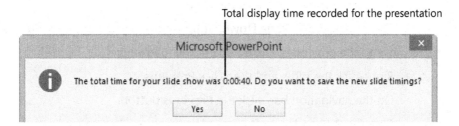

Total display time recorded for the presentation

If- your computer has two monitors, or if you will be presenting a slide show from your computer on a separate display device, you can control the presentation on one monitor and display the slides to the audience on the second monitor or display device. You can use Presenter view to display the current slide, slide notes, next slide, and slide controls in one window, whether on the same monitor or on a separate monitor.

While delivering a presentation, you can direct attention to specific content by using the on-screen pointer, or reinforce your message by drawing or highlighting specific text on slides.

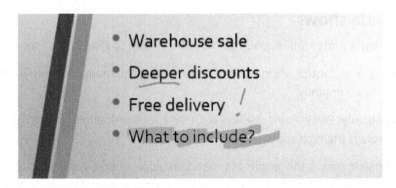

The pen color is determined by a setting in the Set Up Show dialog box, but you can easily change the pen color during the presentation.

➤ **To move between slides**

→ To move to the next slide, do any of the following:

- ○ Click the current slide.
- ○ Right-click the slide, and then click **Next**.
- ○ On the navigation bar, click the **Next** button.
- ○ Click the **N, Enter, Page Down, Right Arrow, Down Arrow,** or **Spacebar** key.

→ To move to the previous slide, do any of the following:

- ○ Right-click the slide, and then click **Previous**.
- ○ On the navigation bar, click the **Previous** button.
- ○ Click the **P, Page Up, Left Arrow, Up Arrow,** or **Backspace** key.

→ To move to a specific slide, do any of the following:

- ○ Enter the slide number, and then press **Enter**.
- ○ In **Presenter** view, click the **See All Slides** button, and then click the slide.
- ○ To return to the beginning of the presentation, point to the presentation screen, and then press and hold both mouse buttons for two seconds.

➤ **To record slide timings**

1. Display the first slide of the presentation.
2. On the **Slide Show** tab, in the **Set Up** group, click the **Rehearse Timings** button.
3. Rehearse the presentation, advancing the slides at the appropriate times.
4. When the slide show ends, click **Yes** in the **Microsoft PowerPoint** dialog box that opens, to apply the recorded slide timings to the slides.

> **Tip** To repeat the rehearsal for a particular slide, on the Recording toolbar, click the Repeat button to reset the time for that slide to 0:00:00. To start the entire rehearsal over again, click the Recording toolbar's Close button, and then when a message asks whether you want to keep the existing timings, click No.

➤ **To deliver a presentation on one monitor and use Presenter view on another**

1. In the **Set Up Show** dialog box, in the **Multiple monitors** area, in the **Slide show monitor** list, click the monitor on which you want to display the slides to the audience.

2. Select the **Show Presenter View** check box, and then click **OK**.

3. Switch to **Slide Show** view. Then on the control monitor, use the **Presenter** view tools to control the presentation.

   Or

1. On the **Slide Show** tab, in the **Monitors** group, in the **Show Presentation On** list, click the monitor on which you want to display the slides to the audience.

2. In the **Monitors** group, select the **Use Presenter View** check box.

3. Switch to **Slide Show** view. Then on the control monitor, use the **Presenter** view tools to control the presentation.

➤ **To use an on-screen pen, highlighter, or laser pointer**

➜ To change the pointer to a pen, press **Ctrl+P**.

➜ To change the pointer to an arrow, press **Ctrl+A**. Or

   Or

1. In **Slide Show** view, on the navigation toolbar, click the **Pen** button, and then click **Pen**, **Highlighter**, or **Laser Pointer**.

   Or

   Right-click anywhere on the screen, click **Pointer Options**, and then click **Pen**, **Highlighter**, or **Laser Pointer**.

> **Tip** Right-clicking the screen displays a shortcut menu only if the Show Menu On Right Mouse Click check box is selected on the Advanced page of the PowerPoint Options dialog box.

2. Use the tool to annotate the slide or draw attention to specific content.

3. Turn off the tool by changing the pointer to an arrow.

> **Tip** When the pen, highlighter, or laser pointer tool is active in Slide Show view, clicking the mouse button does not advance the slide show to the next slide. You need to switch back to the regular pointer to use the mouse to advance the slide.

Practice tasks

The practice file for these tasks is located in the MOSPowerPoint2013\Objective1 practice file folder. Save the results of the tasks in the same folder.

- Open the *PowerPoint_1-5* presentation, and complete the following tasks:
  - ○ Create a custom slide show named *Managers* that includes slides 1, 3, 4, 5, 7, and 10.
  - ○ Edit the Managers slide show to add slide 11.
  - ○ Display the presentation in Slide Show view. Set the pen color to bright blue, and then underline the word *shared* on slide 3.
  - ○ On slide 3, erase the line under the word *shared*. Then highlight the word in light green.
  - ○ On slide 6, use a red pen to draw circles around the two instances of *External* and the word *internal*.
  - ○ End the slide show and retain the annotations.
  - ○ Save the presentation as *MyNotes.pptx*.

Objective review

Before finishing this chapter, ensure that you have mastered the following skills:

1.1   Create presentations
1.2   Format presentations by using slide masters
1.3   Customize presentation options and views
1.4   Configure presentations to print or save
1.5   Configure and present slide shows

2 Insert and format slides and shapes

The skills tested in this section of the Microsoft Office Specialist exam for Microsoft PowerPoint 2013 relate to inserting and formatting slides within a presentation, and inserting and formatting shapes on slides. Specifically, the following objectives are associated with this set of skills:

2.1 Insert and format slides

2.2 Insert and format shapes

2.3 Order and group shapes and slides

After creating a PowerPoint presentation, you can modify it in many ways. You can add slides, remove slides, and hide slides that you don't want to include when displaying the presentation as a slide show. You can also add shapes to slides to enhance their content or illustrate specific concepts.

This chapter guides you in studying ways of adding, removing, and hiding slides within an existing presentation; formatting slide backgrounds; inserting, formatting, and arranging shapes; adding text to shapes; creating presentation sections; and reordering slides within a presentation.

Practice Files To complete the practice tasks in this chapter, you need the practice files contained in the MOSPowerPoint2013\Objective2 practice file folder. For more information, see "Download the practice files" in this book's Introduction.

2.1 Insert and format slides

Add, remove, and hide slides

When you insert a slide into a presentation, PowerPoint inserts it with the default layout immediately after the current slide. If you want to add a slide with a different layout, you select the layout you want from the New Slide gallery. The available layouts and their design depend on the template used to create the presentation.

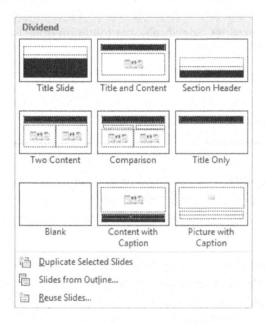

After you insert a slide, you can change its layout at any time. For more information, see section 1.2, "Format presentations by using slide masters."

If you want to insert a slide that is similar to an existing slide, you can duplicate the existing slide and then change it instead of having to create the slide from scratch.

If you decide not to include a slide when you deliver a presentation but you don't want to delete the slide entirely, you can hide the slide. Then PowerPoint will skip over that slide during delivery. Hidden slides are still visible in Normal view and Slide Sorter view, but they appear shaded and have a slash through the slide number.

Hidden slide

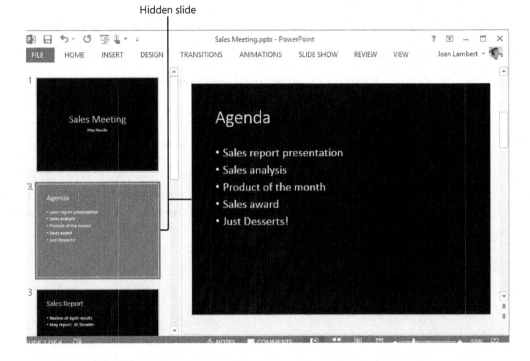

➤ **To add slides**

→ In **Normal** view or **Slide Sorter** view, click the slide that you want the new slide to follow, and then on the **Home** tab, in the **Slides** group, do one of the following:

- ○ To add a slide of a specific layout, click the **New Slide** arrow, and then click the slide layout you want to add.

- ○ To add a slide of the currently selected layout, click the **New Slide** button or press **Ctrl+M**.

- ○ To add a slide that is identical to the currently selected slide, click the **New Slide** arrow, and then click **Duplicate Selected Slides**.

→ Right-click a slide, and then do one of the following:

- ○ To add a slide of the currently selected layout, click **New Slide**.

- ○ To add a slide that is identical to the currently selected slide, click **Duplicate Slide**.

➤ **To delete slides**

→ Right-click a slide or selected slides, and then click **Delete Slide**.

➤ **To hide slides**

→ Right-click a slide or selected slides, and then click **Hide Slide**.

Format slide backgrounds

In PowerPoint, you can customize the background of a slide by adding a solid color, a color gradient, a texture, or even a picture.

In the Format Background pane, you can control the appearance of the color, texture, pattern, or picture applied to the background of the current slide or slide master.

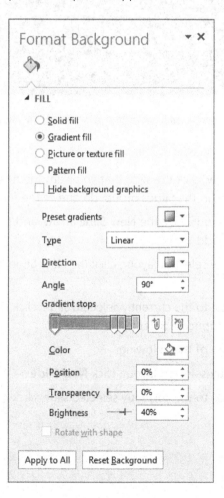

You can configure a simple yet elegant slide background by displaying a solid color or color gradient that reflects the color scheme applied to the presentation.

You can configure a more complex slide background by selecting one of the 15 built-in textures or 48 patterns that can be customized with any two colors.

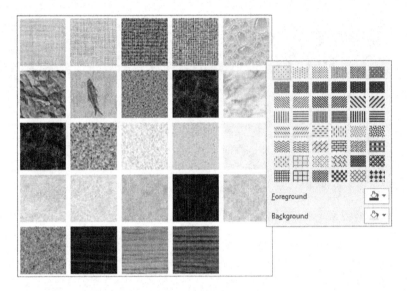

Each texture is a small graphic that is tiled on the slide and designed to repeat gracefully, both horizontally and vertically.

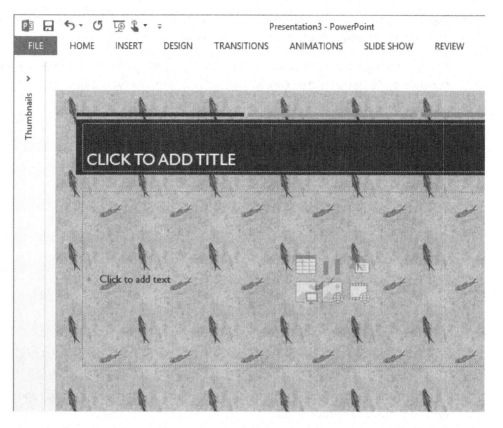

If none of the textures meets your requirements, you can tile a picture of your own. You can customize a slide background even further by using a picture as the background. Because most pictures are too busy to support the inclusion of other content on the slide, these are often best used for title slides or other slides that don't have to support a lot of content.

> **Tip** If you want to add a watermark, such as the word *Draft* or *Confidential*, to the background of your slides, add the text to the background of the slide master.

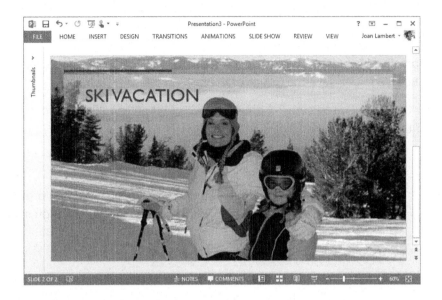

> ➤ **To display the Format Background pane**
>
> → On the **Design** tab, in the **Customize** group, click the **Format Background** button.

> ➤ **To modify slide backgrounds**

1. In the **Format Background** pane, do one of the following:

○ Click **Solid fill**, and then select the color and set the transparency.

○ Click **Gradient fill**, and then select the type, direction, angle, gradient stops, and one or more colors. For each color, set the position, transparency, and brightness.

○ Click **Picture or texture fill**, and then select a local or online picture, or select a texture. Then set the transparency and if appropriate, select the **Tile picture as texture** check box or set the offset, scale, alignment, or mirror type.

○ Click **Pattern fill**, and then select a pattern, foreground color, and background color.

2. If you want to remove the background graphics applied by the slide master, select the **Hide background graphics** check box.

3. If you want to apply the background settings to the slide master, click **Apply to All**.

Practice tasks

The practice file for these tasks is located in the MOSPowerPoint2013\Objective2 practice file folder. Save the results of the tasks in the same folder.

• Open the *PowerPoint_2-1* presentation, and then complete the following tasks:

  ○ Immediately following the title slide, add a new slide with the default Title And Content layout.

  ○ From the New Slide gallery, add one slide of each layout in order, beginning with the Section Header layout, so that the presentation contains a total of nine slides.

  ○ Delete the blank slide (slide 7) from the presentation.

  ○ Hide the Title Only slide (slide 6).

  ○ Format the background of only the Section Header slide (slide 3) with a radial gradient fill that extends from the center of the slide. Set the beginning color to Aqua, Accent 1; set the ending color to Indigo, Accent 2; and remove all interim gradient stops. Accept all other default settings.

  ○ Save the presentation as *MyStarter.pptx*.

2.2 Insert and format shapes

To emphasize, illustrate, or embellish key points in a presentation, you can add simple shapes or complex arrangements of shapes to slides. PowerPoint provides tools for creating several types of shapes, including stars, banners, boxes, lines, circles, and squares. With a little imagination, you can create drawings by combining multiple shapes.

After you draw a shape, or if you select a shape by clicking it, the shape is surrounded by a set of handles. You can change the dimensions, aspect ratio, angles, or rotation of the shape by dragging the handles.

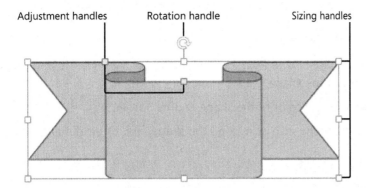

Adjustment handles   Rotation handle   Sizing handles

You can precisely modify the size of a shape by using the commands in the Size group on the Format tool tab, or in the Format Shape pane.

After drawing a shape, you can further modify it by using the commands on the Format tool tab. For example, you can:

- Add text to a shape. PowerPoint centers the text as you enter it, and the text becomes part of the shape.
- Change the size and color of the shape and its border.
- Apply special effects, such as making the shape look three-dimensional.

You can format the shape by selecting a preconfigured set of formatting from the Shape Styles gallery, or by individually formatting the shape fill, outline, and effects. Having made changes to one shape, you can easily apply the same attributes to another shape by using the Format Painter tool.

➤ **To insert shapes**

1. On the **Insert** tab, in the **Illustrations** group, click the **Shapes** button.

2. In the **Shapes** gallery, click the shape you want, and then do one of the following:

    ○ Click on the slide to insert a shape of the default dimensions.

    ○ Drag on the slide to insert a shape of a custom size and shape.

> **Tip** To draw a circle or a square, click the Oval or a Rectangle shape, and hold down the Shift key while you drag.

➤ **To format shapes**

1. Click the shape you want to format. To apply the same formatting to multiple shapes, press and hold the **Ctrl** key, and then click the other shapes.

2. On the **Format** tool tab, in the **Shape Styles** group, select a combination of fill, border, and effects from the **Shape Styles** gallery.

   Or

1. Select the shape or shapes you want to format.

2. In the **Shape Styles** group, click the **Shape Fill** arrow, and then do one of the following:

   ○ To add or change a fill color, click the color you want.

   ○ To choose no color, click **No Fill**.

   ○ To use a color that isn't one of the theme colors, click **More Fill Colors**, and then either click the color that you want on the **Standard** page, or mix your own color on the **Custom** page. Custom colors and colors on the **Standard** page do not update if you later change the document theme.

   ○ To adjust the transparency of the shape, click **More Fill Colors**. At the bottom of the **Colors** dialog box, move the **Transparency** slider, or enter a number in the box next to the slider. You can vary the percentage of transparency from **0%** (fully opaque, the default setting) to **100%** (fully transparent).

   ○ To add or change a fill picture, click **Picture**. In the **Insert Pictures** dialog box, locate the folder that contains the picture that you want to use, click the picture file, and then click **Insert**.

   ○ To add or change a fill gradient, click **Gradient**, and then click the gradient variation you want. To customize the gradient, click **More Gradients** and then, in the **Format Shape** pane, choose the options you want.

   ○ To add or change a fill texture, click **Texture**, and then click the texture you want. To customize the texture, click **More Textures** and then, in the **Format Shape** pane, choose the options that you want.

3. Click the **Shape Outline** arrow, and then select the outline color, weight, style, and endpoints.

4. Click the **Shape Effects** arrow, and then select the shadow, reflection, glow, soft edge, beveled edge, and rotation effects you want.

➤ **To modify shapes**

→ Select the shape to activate the handles, and then do any of the following:

○ Drag the white sizing handles to change the external dimensions of the shape.

○ Drag the yellow adjustment handle or handles to change the internal dimensions of the shape without changing its size.

○ Drag the rotating handle to adjust the angle of rotation of the shape.

➤ **To add formatted text to a shape**

1. Select the shape, and then enter the text.

2. On the **Format** tool tab, in the **WordArt Styles** group, click the **Quick Styles** button if necessary to display the **WordArt** gallery and then, in the **WordArt** gallery, click the text style you want.

Or

On the **Home** tab, in the **Font** group, use the commands to set the font, font size, and font formatting options you want.

3. To modify the text formatting, click the **Text Fill**, **Text Outline**, or **Text Effects** arrow, and then select the formatting options you want.

➤ **To copy formatting from one shape to other shapes**

1. Click the shape from which you want to copy the formatting.

2. On the **Home** tab, in the **Clipboard** group, click the **Format Painter** button once, and then click another shape to copy the formatting to that one shape.

Or

Double-click the **Format Painter** button, click one or more shapes to copy the for-matting to those shapes, and then click the **Format Painter** button or press the **Esc** key to turn off the Format Painter tool.

➤ **To apply the attributes of a shape to all future shapes in the active presentation**

→ Right-click the shape, and then click **Set as Default Shape**.

Practice tasks

The practice file for these tasks is located in the MOSPowerPoint2013\Objective2 practice file folder. Save the results of the tasks in the same folder.

- Open the *PowerPoint_2-2* presentation, and then complete the following tasks:

  - On slide 4, insert Sun, Moon, and Heart shapes at their default sizes.

  - Set the Sun shape to a size of 3" by 3", the Moon shape to a size of 2" by 1.5", and the Heart shape to a size of 2" by 2".

  - Rotate the Moon shape exactly 180 degrees so that the open curve is on the left and the outer curve is on the right.

  - Apply a 1-point, white outline to all three shapes.

  - Fill the Sun shape with Yellow, the Moon shape with Orange, and the Heart shape with Red (all colors from the Standard Colors palette).

  - Add the word *Nature* to the Sun shape, the word *Sleep* to the Moon shape, and the word *Family* to the Heart shape. Then format the words by applying the first WordArt Quick Style (Fill – Black, Text 1, Shadow).

  - Flip the Moon shape vertically so that its text is right-side up. Then set the text direction so that the text runs sideways from bottom to top.

  - Save the presentation as *MyShapes.pptx*.

2.3 Order and group shapes and slides

Arrange slide content

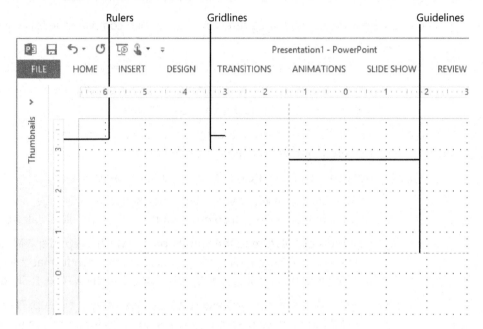

PowerPoint 2013 has several tools that help you to arrange content on a slide or slide master:

- The horizontal and vertical rulers measure the distance from the center of a slide.

- Gridlines are fixed indicators that mark a grid of the size you select by using major and minor indicators. The default gridlines mark off half-inch squares, with indicators every 1/12 inch. You can have PowerPoint snap objects to the grid regardless of whether the grid is currently displayed.

- Guides are movable indicators that help you to align objects with other objects.

- Smart guides appear when the object you're moving is aligned with the edge or centerline of another object, is equidistant from two points, or reflects the spacing of a parallel object.

You can turn all of these indicators on or off in the Grid And Guides dialog box.

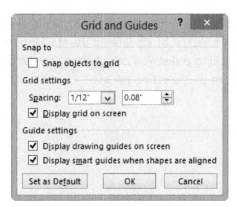

After inserting pictures or drawing shapes in the approximate locations you want them on a slide, you can align them and change their stacking order. You can use the automatic alignment commands to align individual or multiple graphics in several ways. For example, you can:

- Align graphics vertically by the left or right edges or centerline, or horizontally by the top or bottom edges or centerline.
- Distribute graphics evenly within their current space, either horizontally or vertically.
- Align graphics relative to the slide that contains them or to other selected objects.

> **Tip** If you add pictures to a slide by clicking the Pictures button in the Images group on the Insert tab, you can group them and then align and position them as a group the same way you would group shapes. However, if you add them by clicking the Pictures button in separate content placeholders, you cannot group them.

When you have multiple shapes on a slide, you can group them so that you can copy, move, and format them as a unit. You can change the attributes of an individual shape—for example, its color, size, or location—without ungrouping the shapes. If you do ungroup them, you can easily regroup the same selection of shapes.

Regardless of whether graphics and other slide elements actually overlap each other, all the elements on an individual slide are stacked in a specific order. The default stacking order is determined by the order in which elements are inserted. Opaque elements (such as graphics, filled shapes, and filled text boxes) that are later in the stacking order can hide elements that are earlier in the stacking order. You can change the stacking order from an element's shortcut menu or from the Selection pane.

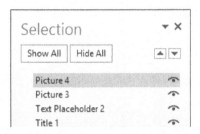

> **Tip** If you can't select an object on a slide because it is covered by another, select and reorder the object from within the Selection pane. PowerPoint assigns names to objects on the slide; you can change the default names to more descriptive names.

If your presentation must be compatible with assistive technology devices that make presentations accessible to people with disabilities, you should check the order assigned to objects in the Selection pane to ensure that they are in a logical tab or reading order. If necessary, adjust the order by using the Bring Forward or Send Backward arrows.

➤ To display or hide rulers

→ On the **View** tab, in the **Show** group, select or clear the **Ruler** check box.

→ Press **Shift+Alt+F9**.

➤ To display or hide gridlines

→ On the **View** tab, in the **Show** group, select or clear the **Gridlines** check box.

→ Press **Shift+F9**.

➤ **To manage gridlines and guidelines**

1. On the **View** tab, click the **Show** dialog box launcher.

2. In the **Grid and Guides** dialog box, select the check boxes of the features you want to turn on.

3. In the **Spacing** list, select standard grid spacing from **1/24"** to **2"**, or click **Custom**, enter specific spacing in the adjacent box, and then click **OK**.

➤ **To display the Selection pane**

→ On the **Home** tab, in the **Editing** group, click **Select**, and then click **Selection Pane**.

➤ **To align shapes**

1. On the slide or in the **Selection** pane, select one or more shapes you want to align with the slide.

2. On the **Align** menu, if **Align to Slide** is not selected, click that option. Then on the **Align** menu, click **Align Left**, **Align Center**, **Align Right**, **Align Top**, **Align Middle**, or **Align Bottom**.

Or

1. Select two or more shapes you want to align with each other.

2. On the **Format** tool tab, in the **Arrange** group, click the **Align** button. With **Align Selected Objects** selected at the bottom of the menu, click **Align Left**, **Align Center**, **Align Right**, **Align Top**, **Align Middle**, or **Align Bottom**.

Or

With the Smart Guides feature turned on, drag a shape until the smart guide indicates that it is aligned with another.

➤ **To distribute shapes evenly within the current container**

1. Select three or more shapes you want to distribute.

2. On the **Align** menu, click **Distribute Horizontally** or **Distribute Vertically**.

➤ **To group shapes**

1. Select two or more shapes you want to group.

2. On the **Format** tool tab, in the **Arrange** group, click the **Group Objects** button, and then click **Group**.

   Or

   Right-click the selection, click **Group**, and then click **Group**.

➤ **To ungroup shapes**

1. Select grouped shapes by clicking the outer selection outline.

2. On the **Group Objects** menu, click **Ungroup**.

   Or

   Right-click the selection, click **Group**, and then click **Ungroup**.

➤ **To regroup shapes**

➜ Select one shape from the original group. Then on the **Group Objects** menu, click **Regroup**.

➤ **To change the stacking order of shapes**

1. Select one or more shapes you want to move.

2. Right-click the selection, and then do one of the following:

   ○ Click **Bring to Front**, and then click **Bring to Front** to position the selection first in the stacking order.

   ○ Click **Bring to Front**, and then click **Bring Forward** to move the selection one position forward.

   ○ Click **Send to Back**, and then click **Send to Back** to position the selection last in the stacking order.

   ○ Click **Send to Back**, and then click **Send Backward** to move the selection one position backward.

   Or

   In the **Selection** pane, click the **Bring Forward** or **Move Backward** button.

Manage slide order and sections

To make it easier to organize and format a longer presentation, you can divide it into sections. In both Normal view and Slide Sorter view, sections are designated by titles above the first slide in the section. Section titles do not appear in other views.

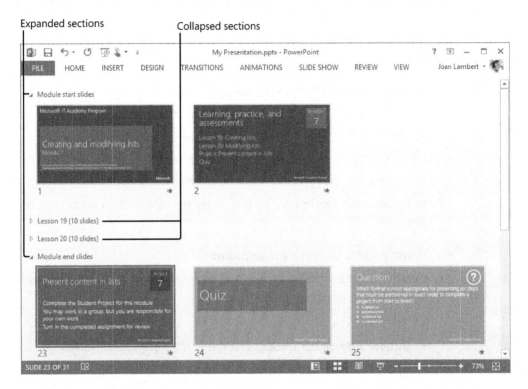

You can select, format, move, collapse, expand, and remove sections of slides by selecting the section title and then performing the action. You can print selected sections of a presentation. When collaborating on the creation of a presentation, individual people can edit separate sections.

You can easily reorder the slides within a presentation by moving individual slides or entire sections of slides.

> **Tip** If you arrange open presentation windows side by side, you can drag slides from one presentation to another.

➤ **To create presentation sections**

   1. In **Normal** view, click in the **Slides** pane above the first slide of the new section.

   Or

   In **Slide Sorter** view, click in the **Slides** pane to the left of first slide of the new section.

   2. On the **Home** tab, in the **Slides** group, click the **Section** button, and then click **Add Section**.

➤ **To rename presentation sections**

   1. Click the section header. On the **Home** tab, in the **Slides** group, click the **Section** button, and then click **Rename Section**.

   Or

   Right-click the section header, and then click **Rename Section**.

   2. In the **Rename Section** dialog box, enter the new section name, and then click **Rename**.

➤ **To move slides within a presentation**

   1. In **Normal** view or **Slide Sorter** view, select the section headers or thumbnails of the slides you want to move.

   Or

   In **Outline** view, select the icons of the slides you want to move.

   2. Drag the selection to the new location.

   Or

   Cut the slides from the original location, and then paste them in the new location.

Practice tasks

The practice file for these tasks is located in the MOSPowerPoint2013\Objective2 practice file folder. Save the results of the tasks in the same folder.

- Open the *PowerPoint_2-3* presentation, and then complete the following tasks:

    - ○ Select the three shapes on slide 4 and align them in the middle and center of the slide.

    - ○ Change the stacking order so that the Heart is in front, the Sun is second, and the Moon is in back.

    - ○ Distribute the three shapes horizontally on the slide. Then group them.

    - ○ Reorder the slides so that slide 3 (the section opener) appears after the title slide, and slide 4 (which contains the shapes) is next.

    - ○ Divide the presentation into three sections, with Section 1 containing only the title slide, Section 2 containing slides 2 through 4, and Section 3 containing slides 5 through 9. Set the name of Section 1 to *Title*, Section 2 to *Overview*, and Section 3 to *Body*.

    - ○ Save the presentation as *MyPresentation.pptx*.

Objective review

Before finishing this chapter, ensure that you have mastered the following skills:

2.1   Insert and format slides

2.2   Insert and format shapes

2.3   Order and group shapes and slides

3 Create slide content

The skills tested in this section of the Microsoft Office Specialist exam for Microsoft PowerPoint 2013 relate to creating slide content. Specifically, the following objectives are associated with this set of skills:

- **3.1** Insert and format text
- **3.2** Insert and format tables
- **3.3** Insert and format charts
- **3.4** Insert and format SmartArt
- **3.5** Insert and format images
- **3.6** Insert and format media

Chapter 2, "Insert and format slides and shapes," introduced you to ways of using shapes on a slide to illustrate or decorate slide content. Traditionally, much slide content has consisted of bullet points. To make the content of slides more interesting and informative, and to allow the slide presenter to engage with and educate the audience, more and more frequently PowerPoint users are communicating information by using more sophisticated elements.

Conveying numeric data effectively in a presentation is especially difficult. If you have a small set of data, you can display the raw values in a formatted table. If you have a large set of data, you can depict relationships or trends by using a chart.

This chapter guides you in studying ways of inserting and formatting text, tables, charts, SmartArt graphics, images, audio clips, and video clips onto slides—in short, all the slide content you'll ever need!

> **Practice Files** To complete the practice tasks in this chapter, you need the practice files contained in the MOSPowerPoint2013\Objective3 practice file folder. For more information, see "Download the practice files" in this book's Introduction.

3.1 Insert and format text

Format text in placeholders

When you add a new slide to a presentation, the layout you choose uses placeholders to indicate the type and position of the objects on the slide. You can enter text directly into a text placeholder on a slide when you're working in Normal view, or you can enter it in the Outline pane when you're working in Outline view.

The default formatting of text in placeholders reflects the design of the underlying slide master. However, you can use standard character and paragraph formatting techniques to override the following aspects of the design:

- **Alignment** You can align the text horizontally to the left, right, or center; or you can justify it to span the text box. You can align the text vertically at the top of the text box, in the middle, or at the bottom.

- **Case** You can make selected text all lowercase or all uppercase; ensure that the text is capitalized as a sentence or that each word has an initial capital letter; or change the capitalization of each letter.

- **Character spacing** You can make the space between characters looser or tighter.

- **Color** Picking a color from the applied color scheme creates a pleasing design impact. You can also add colors that are not part of the color scheme, including colors from the standard palette or from the almost infinite spectrum of colors available in the Colors dialog box.

- **Direction** You can rotate text or stack the letters on top of each other.

- **Fancy text effects** You can apply fancy effects such as shadows, reflections, and bevels, or rotate or mold text into a shape.

- **Font and size** You can pick a different font or size for any selection.

- **Indentation** You can indent the text from the left side of the text box.

- **Line and paragraph spacing** You can adjust the spacing within and between paragraphs.

- **Style and effects** You can apply simple styles such as bold and italic, or you can choose more dramatic effects such as shadows, colored underlining, or small caps.

> **Strategy** PowerPoint responds differently to the way you enter text depending on where you are entering it. Become familiar with the different ways of creating new text and bulleted list levels so that you can enter text efficiently during the exam.

After you format one text selection to suit your needs, you can quickly apply the same combination of formatting to another selection by using the Format Painter. You can also clear all manual formatting from a selection so that it reverts to the formatting specified by the design.

➤ **To create a new line of text with the same style and at the same level as the current one**

→ Press **Enter**.

➤ **To demote the current line of text to the next lower level**

→ Click to the left of the current line, and then press **Tab**.

→ On the **Home** tab, in the **Paragraph** group, click the **Increase List Level** button.

➤ **To promote the current line of text to the next higher level**

→ Click to the left of the current line, and then press **Shift+Tab**.

→ On the **Home** tab, in the **Paragraph** group, click the **Decrease List Level** button.

➤ **To change the font of selected text**

→ On the **Mini Toolbar** or in the **Font** group on the **Home** tab, click the font you want in the **Font** list.

➤ **To increase or decrease the size of selected text**

→ On the **Mini Toolbar** or in the **Font** group on the **Home** tab, click the **Increase Font Size** or **Decrease Font Size** button.

➤ **To precisely size selected text**

→ On the **Mini Toolbar** or in the **Font** group on the **Home** tab, click the size you want on the **Font Size** list.

➤ **To change the case of selected text**

→ On the **Home** tab, in the **Font** group, click the **Change Case** button, and then click the option you want.

➤ **To change the color of selected text**

→ On the **Mini Toolbar** or in the **Font** group on the **Home** tab, click the color you want in the **Font Color** palette.

Or

1. Display the **Font Color** palette, and then click **More Colors**.

2. On either the **Standard** or **Custom** page of the **Colors** dialog box, specify the color you want, and then click **OK**.

➤ **To change the font style or effect of selected text**

→ On the **Mini Toolbar** or in the **Font** group on the **Home** tab, click the button for the style you want.

Or

1. On the **Home** tab, click the **Font** dialog box launcher.

2. In the **Font** dialog box, specify the style or effect you want, and then click **OK**.

➤ **To change the character spacing of selected text**

→ On the **Home** tab, in the **Font** group, click the **Character Spacing** button, and then click **Very Tight**, **Tight**, **Normal**, **Loose**, or **Very Loose**.

Or

1. On the **Home** tab, in the **Font** group, click the **Character Spacing** button, and then click **More Spacing**.

2. On the **Character Spacing** page of the **Font** dialog box, in the **Spacing** list, click **Normal**, **Expanded**, or **Condensed**.

3. Change the **By** setting to the precise amount of space you want between characters, and then click **OK**.

➤ **To change the alignment of selected text**

→ On the **Mini Toolbar** or in the **Paragraph** group on the **Home** tab, click the **Align Left**, **Center**, **Align Right**, or **Justify** button.

→ Press **Ctrl+L** to left-align text, **Ctrl+E** to center text, **Ctrl+R** to right-align text, or **Ctrl+J** to justify text.

→ On the **Home** tab, in the **Paragraph** group, click the **Align Text** button, and then click the vertical alignment you want.

➤ **To change the indentation of selected text**

→ On the **Mini Toolbar** or in the **Paragraph** group on the **Home** tab, click the **Increase List Level** or **Decrease List Level** button.

Or

1. On the **Home** tab, click the **Paragraph** dialog box launcher.
2. In the **Paragraph** dialog box, in the **Indentation** area, change the **Before text** setting, and then click **OK**.

➤ **To change the line spacing of selected text**

→ On the **Home** tab, in the **Paragraph** group, click the **Line Spacing** button, and then click the spacing you want.

> **Tip** Clicking Line Spacing Options displays the Paragraph dialog box.

Or

1. On the **Home** tab, click the **Paragraph** dialog box launcher.
2. In the **Paragraph** dialog box, in the **Spacing** area, change the **Before** or **After** settings, or the **Line Spacing** option, and then click **OK**.

➤ **To change the direction of text in a placeholder**

→ Click anywhere in the placeholder, and on the **Home** tab, in the **Paragraph** group, click the **Text Direction** button, and then click the direction you want.

➤ **To copy the formatting of selected text**

1. On the **Mini Toolbar** or in the **Clipboard** group of the **Home** tab, click the **Format Painter** button.
2. Select the text to which you want to apply the formatting.

➤ **To copy the formatting of selected text multiple times**

1. On the **Mini Toolbar** or in the **Clipboard** group on the **Home** tab, double-click the **Format Painter** button.
2. Select the text to which you want to apply the formatting.
3. When you finish applying the formatting, click the **Format Painter** button to deactivate it.

➤ **To clear all manual formatting from selected text**

→ On the **Home** tab, in the **Font** group, click the **Clear All Formatting** button.
→ Press **Ctrl+Spacebar**.

Create WordArt

WordArt provides a method for applying a series of effects to text content. These effects can include outlines, fills, shadows, reflections, glow effects, beveled edges, and three-dimensional rotation. You can use one of the 20 default WordArt styles, modify the effects applied to a WordArt object, or build a combination of effects from scratch.

Become a Microsoft Office Specialist!

➤ **To create a WordArt object**

1. On the **Insert** tab, in the **Text** group, click the **WordArt** button, and then click the style you want.

> **Tip** To create a WordArt object from existing text, select the text before you click the WordArt button.

2. If necessary, replace the placeholder text in the WordArt object.

3. Set the size and other attributes of the text as you would with any other text.

➤ **To format the background of a selected WordArt object**

→ On the **Format** tool tab, do any of the following:

   ○ In the **Shape Styles** gallery, click the built-in style you want to apply.

   ○ In the **Shape Styles** group, in the **Shape Fill**, **Shape Outline**, and **Shape Effects** galleries, click the settings you want.

➤ **To format the text of a selected WordArt object**

→ On the **Format** tool tab, do any of the following:

   ○ In the **WordArt Styles** gallery, click the built-in style you want to apply.

   ○ In the **WordArt Styles** group, in the **Text Fill**, **Text Outline**, and **Text Effects** galleries, click the settings you want.

> **Tip** You change the size, shape, and location of a WordArt object by using the same techniques that you use with other graphic elements.

Format text as columns

When a slide includes several short entries, they can look better and be easier to read when presented in multiple columns. Some slide layouts include text placeholders for multiple columns of text. However, you can format text within any placeholder into multiple columns.

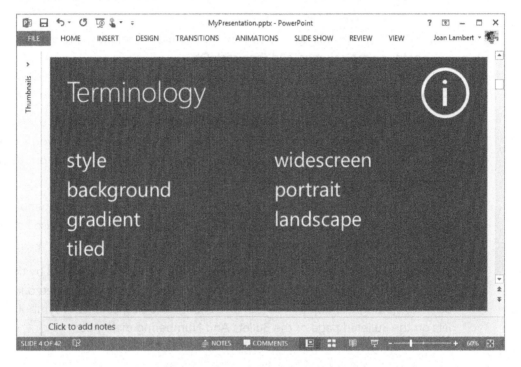

The width of the columns is determined by the width of the text placeholder, the number of columns, and the spacing between the columns. You can format text into one, two, or three columns spaced a half inch apart by selecting the number of columns from a list, or you can format text into up to 16 columns by specifying the number and spacing of the columns in the Columns dialog box.

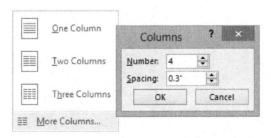

> ➤ **To format selected text in columns**

→ On the **Home** tab, in the **Paragraph** group, click the **Add or Remove Columns** button, and then click **One Column**, **Two Columns**, or **Three Columns**.

Or

1. On the **Home** tab, in the **Paragraph** group, click the **Add or Remove Columns** button, and then click **More Columns**.

2. In the **Columns** dialog box, specify the number of columns and the spacing between the columns, and then click **OK**.

Format text as lists

Bulleted lists form the foundation of most presentations. You can enter up to nine levels of bullets in a content placeholder. By default, the bulleted list items you enter are all first level, but you can easily demote and promote list item levels, both on the slide and in Outline view.

If you have entered regular text paragraphs in a placeholder or an independent text box, you can convert the text to a bulleted list or a numbered list. You can also convert a bulleted list or numbered list to regular text paragraphs.

The appearance of the bullet characters for each list level is determined by the formatting prescribed on the slide master. However, you can customize a bulleted list by using basic formatting techniques. You can also change the size, color, and symbol of the bullets on the Bulleted page of the Bullets And Numbering dialog box.

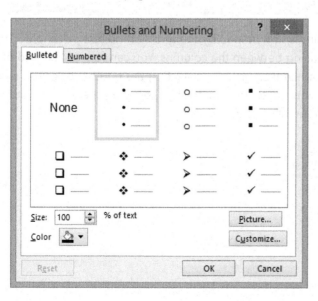

For a numbered list, you can change the number scheme and the size and color of the numbers on the Numbered page of the Bullets And Numbering dialog box.

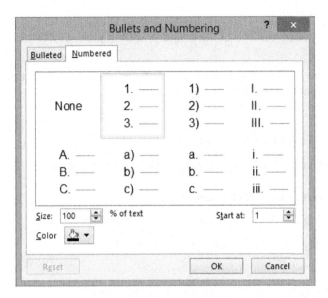

For both types of lists, you can specify the indenting of each level. If you want to adjust the indenting of multiple levels, it is best to start with the lowest level and work your way up, using equal increments. Otherwise you might end up with a list that looks uneven and unprofessional.

> **See Also** For information about formatting bulleted list items as SmartArt diagrams, see section 3.4, "Insert and format SmartArt."

➤ **To demote a bulleted list item**

→ With the cursor in the bulleted list item, on the **Home** tab, in the **Paragraph** group, click the **Increase List Level** button.

→ Click to the left of the text of the bullet point, and then press the **Tab** key.

> **Tip** In the Outline pane, you can also use these techniques to change a slide title to a bulleted list item or demote a numbered list item to a lower level.

➤ **To promote a bulleted list item**

→ With the cursor in the list item, on the **Home** tab, in the **Paragraph** group, click the **Decrease List Level** button.

→ Click to the left of the text of the bullet point, and then press **Shift+Tab**.

> **Tip** In the Outline pane, you can also use these techniques to change a bullet point to a slide title or promote a numbered item to a higher level.

➤ **To convert selected text to a bulleted list**

→ On the **Home** tab, in the **Paragraph** group, click the **Bullets** button.

➤ **To change the bullets in a selected bulleted list**

1. On the **Home** tab, in the **Paragraph** group, click the **Bullets** arrow.

2. In the **Bullets** gallery, click the bullet style you want.

   Or

1. Display the **Bullets** gallery, and click **Bullets and Numbering**.

2. On the **Bulleted** page of the **Bullets and Numbering** dialog box, change the size and color of the existing bullet.

3. To change the bullet symbol, click **Customize**, choose a font and symbol in the **Symbol** dialog box, and then click **OK**.

4. To use a picture as a bullet, click **Picture**, and then in the **Insert Picture** dialog box, locate and double-click the picture file you want.

5. Click **OK** to close the **Bullets and Numbering** dialog box.

➤ **To convert selected text to a numbered list**

→ On the **Home** tab, in the **Paragraph** group, click the **Numbering** button.

➤ **To change the numbers in a selected numbered list**

1. On the **Home** tab, in the **Paragraph** group, click the **Numbering** arrow.

2. In the **Numbering** gallery, click the number scheme you want.

   Or

1. In the **Numbering** gallery, click **Bullets and Numbering**.

2. On the **Numbered** page of the **Bullets and Numbering** dialog box, change the size and color of the numbers, and then click **OK**.

> **To adjust the hanging indent of a list**

→ Drag the **First Line Indent** and **Hanging Indent** markers to the left or right on the ruler.

> **Tip** To display the ruler, select the Ruler check box in the Show group on the View tab.

Format text as hyperlinks

Presentations that are intended to be viewed electronically often include hyperlinks to provide access to supporting information. That information might be on a hidden slide, in another presentation, in a file on your computer or your organization's network, or on a website. If you use Microsoft Outlook, you can also use a hyperlink to open an email message window so that people viewing the presentation can easily contact you.

You can attach a hyperlink to any selected object, such as text, a graphic, a shape, or a table. Clicking the hyperlinked object then takes you directly to the linked location. Editing the object does not disrupt the hyperlink; however, deleting the object also deletes the hyperlink.

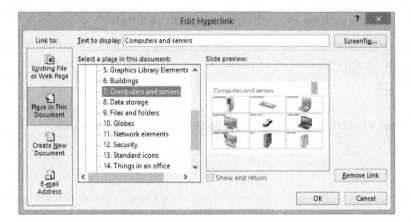

> **To link a selected object to a slide**

1. Press **Ctrl+K** or, on the **Insert** tab, in the **Links** group, click the **Hyperlink** button.

2. In the **Insert Hyperlink** dialog box, in the **Link to** area, click **Place in This Document**.

3. In the **Select a place in this document** list, click the slide you want, and then click **OK**.

➤ **To link a selected object to a file**

1. In the **Insert Hyperlink** or **Edit Hyperlink** dialog box, in the **Link to** area, click **Existing File or Web Page**.

2. Do one of the following, and then click **OK**:

   ○ With **Current Folder** selected, locate and click the file you want.

   ○ Click **Recent Files** and then, in the list, click the file you want.

➤ **To link a selected object to a webpage**

1. In the **Insert Hyperlink** dialog box, and in the **Link to** area, click **Existing File or Web Page**.

2. Do one of the following, and then click **OK**:

   ○ In the **Address** box, enter the URL of the webpage.

   ○ Click **Browsed Pages** and then, in the list, click the URL you want.

➤ **To link a selected object to an email message form**

1. In the **Insert Hyperlink** or **Edit Hyperlink** dialog box, in the **Link to** area, click **E-mail Address**.

2. In the **E-mail address** box, enter the recipient's address.

3. If you want to automatically populate the **Subject** field of the email message created by clicking the hyperlink, enter the subject in the **Subject** box.

4. Click **OK**.

Tip To test a hyperlink, you must be in Slide Show view or Reading view.

Practice tasks

The practice file for these tasks is located in the MOSPowerPoint2013\Objective3 practice file folder. Save the results of the tasks in the same folder.

- Open the *PowerPoint_3-1* presentation, and then perform the following tasks:
  - ○ On slide 2, format the title as bold, purple, and small caps. Adjust the character spacing so that it is very loose. Then apply the same formatting to the titles of all the other slides.
  - ○ On slide 2, convert the bulleted list items to normal paragraphs. Format the paragraphs in two columns, and then resize the placeholder so that the columns are of equal length.
  - ○ On slide 2, create a hyperlink from each paragraph that has a corresponding page in the presentation to that page.
  - ○ On slide 3, increase the hanging indent of the second-level list items to a half inch.
  - ○ On slide 6, create an independent text box containing the text *Be sure to check the manual for important information about the minimum requirements*. Format the text as italic, and then adjust the size of the text box so that the text wraps on multiple lines.
  - ○ On slide 6, change the bullets to dark red dollar signs.
  - ○ On slide 8, change the second-level list to a numbered list, and then set the numbering scheme to use purple capital letters.

3.2 Insert and format tables

Create and import tables

When you want to present a lot of data in an organized and easy-to-read format, a table is often your best choice. You can create a table in one of the following ways:

- Have PowerPoint insert a table with the number of columns and rows you specify.
- Draw the table by dragging on the slide to create cells that are the size and shape you need.
- If the table already exists in a Microsoft Word document or Microsoft Excel workbook, you can copy and paste that table onto a slide rather than re-create it.

If you want to use data from an Excel worksheet in a PowerPoint table, you can do any of the following:

- Copy and paste the data as a table.
- Embed the worksheet on a slide as an object.
- Link the slide to the worksheet so that the slide reflects any changes you make to the worksheet data.

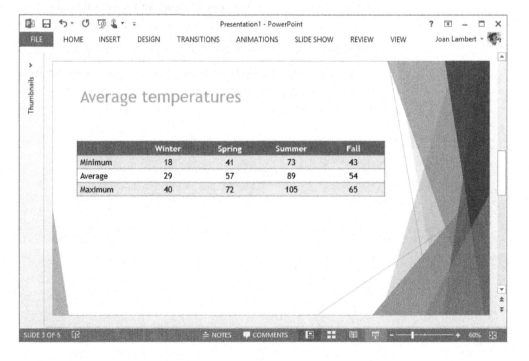

To enter information in a table, you simply click a cell and then enter text. You can also move the insertion point from cell to cell by pressing the Tab key.

When a table is active on a slide, the Design and Layout tool tabs are available on the ribbon.

➤ To create a new table

1. In a content placeholder, click the **Insert Table** button.
2. In the **Insert Table** dialog box, specify the number of columns and rows, and then click **OK**.
3. Enter or copy and paste the information into the table structure.

   Or

1. On the **Insert** tab, in the **Tables** group, click the **Table** button.
2. Move the pointer across and down the grid to select the number of columns and rows you want, and then click the lower-right cell in the selection.
3. Enter or copy and paste the information into the table structure.

➤ To draw a table

1. On the **Insert** tab, in the **Tables** group, click the **Table** button, and then click **Draw Table**.
2. Position the pencil cursor, and drag down and to the right to create a cell the size you want.
3. On the **Design** tool tab, in the **Draw Borders** group, click the **Draw Table** button, and then draw the next cell.
4. Repeat step 3 to draw as many cells as you need.
5. Enter the information into the table structure.

➤ To insert a table from Word

1. In the source document, click the table border to select it.
2. Copy the table to the Microsoft Office Clipboard.
3. Switch to PowerPoint, display the destination slide, and then paste the table from the Clipboard.

➤ **To paste Excel data as a table**

1. In the Excel worksheet, select and copy the data you want to display in the PowerPoint table.

2. Switch to PowerPoint, display the destination slide, and then paste the data.

3. To change the default paste option (Use Destination Styles), click the **Paste Options** button, and then click the option you want.

➤ **To embed an editable worksheet**

1. In the Excel worksheet, select and copy the data you want to display on the PowerPoint slide.

2. Switch to PowerPoint, display the destination slide, click the **Paste Options** button, and then click **Embed**.

   Or

1. In the workbook that contains the worksheet, ensure that the worksheet you want to embed is the active worksheet, and then save and close the workbook.

2. On the **Insert** tab, in the **Text** group, click the **Object** button.

3. In the **Insert Object** dialog box, click **Create from file**, and then click **Browse**.

4. In the **Browse** dialog box, locate and double-click the workbook, and then click **OK**.

➤ **To eliminate extraneous columns and rows**

1. Double-click the worksheet object.

2. When the worksheet opens in an Excel window within PowerPoint, size the frame around the worksheet so that it is just big enough to contain the active part of the worksheet.

3. Click outside the frame to return to PowerPoint.

➤ **To resize the worksheet**

→ Point to any handle (the sets of dots) around the worksheet object, and then drag to enlarge or shrink it.

➤ **To modify an embedded worksheet**

1. Double-click the worksheet object.

2. Use Excel techniques to edit and format the embedded object.

➤ **To link to a worksheet**

→ Follow the instructions for embedding a worksheet, but in the **Insert Object** dialog box, select the **Link** check box before clicking **OK**.

➤ **To update a linked worksheet**

→ Double-click the table on the slide to open the linked worksheet in Excel, make the changes, and then save them.

→ If you update the linked worksheet in Excel and want to synchronize the table on the slide, right-click the table on the slide, and then click **Update Link**.

➤ **To update table data**

→ Use normal editing techniques to change the data in a cell.

➤ **To delete a table**

→ On the **Layout** tool tab, in the **Rows & Columns** group, click the **Delete** button, and then click **Delete Table**.

Change table structure

After you insert a table, you can change its structure in the following ways:

- Add columns or rows.
- Delete columns or rows.
- Combine (merge) selected cells into one cell that spans two or more columns or rows.
- Split a single cell into two or more cells.
- Size columns or rows.
- Size the table.

Seasonal temperature fluctuations			
	Winter	Spring	Summer	Fall
Minimum	18	41	73	43
Average	29	57	89	54
Maximum	40	72	105	65

➤ **To add a row**

→ In the last cell of the last row, press **Tab** to insert a new row at the bottom of the table.

→ On the **Layout** tool tab, in the **Rows & Columns** group, click the **Insert Above** or **Insert Below** button to insert a row above or below the row containing the cursor.

➤ **To add a column**

→ On the **Layout** tool tab, in the **Rows & Columns** group, click the **Insert Left** or **Insert Right** button to insert a column to the left or right of the column containing the cursor.

➤ **To delete a row or column**

→ On the **Layout** tool tab, in the **Rows & Columns** group, click the **Delete** button, and then click **Delete Columns** or **Delete Rows** to delete the row or column containing the cursor.

➤ **To select table elements**

→ To select a cell, point just inside its left border, and then click when the cursor changes to a black arrow pointing up and to the right.

→ To select a column, point above its top border, and then click when the cursor changes to a black downward-pointing arrow.

   Or

   Click a cell in the column, and on the **Layout** tool tab, in the **Table** group, click the **Select** button, and then click **Select Column**.

→ To select a row, point outside the table to the left of the row, and then click when the cursor changes to a black right-pointing arrow.

   Or

   Click a cell in the row, and on the **Layout** tool tab, in the **Table** group, click the **Select** button, and then click **Select Row**.

→ To select multiple cells, columns, or rows, select the first element, and then hold down the **Shift** key as you select subsequent elements.

   Or

   Drag through adjacent cells, columns, or rows.

→ To select an entire table, click any cell, and on the **Layout** tool tab, in the **Table** group, click the **Select** button, and then click **Select Table**.

➤ **To split a cell into two or more cells**

1. Click the cell, and on the **Layout** tool tab, in the **Merge** group, click the **Split Cells** button.

2. In the **Split Cells** dialog box, specify the number of columns and rows you want the cell to be split into, and then click **OK**.

➤ **To merge two or more selected cells in a row or column**

→ Select the cells, and then on the **Layout** tool tab, in the **Merge** group, click the **Merge Cells** button.

Or

1. On the **Design** tool tab, in the **Draw Borders** group, click the **Eraser** button, and then click the borders between the cells you want to merge.

2. Click the **Eraser** button again to turn it off.

➤ **To change the size of a selected element**

→ To change the width of a column, point to the right border of one of its cells, and when the opposing arrows appear, drag the border to the left or right.

Or

On the **Layout** tool tab, in the **Cell Size** group, adjust the **Table Column Width** setting.

→ To size a column to fit its entries, point to the right border of one of its cells, and when the opposing arrows appear, double-click.

→ To change the height of a row, point to the bottom border of one of its cells, and when the opposing arrows appear, drag the border up or down.

Or

On the **Layout** tool tab, in the **Cell Size** group, adjust the **Table Row Height** setting.

→ To evenly distribute the widths of selected columns or the heights of selected rows, on the **Layout** tool tab, in the **Cell Size** group, click the **Distribute Columns** or **Distribute Rows** button.

→ To change the size of a selected table, point to any handle (the sets of dots) around its frame, and then drag in the direction you want the table to grow or shrink.

Or

On the **Layout** tool tab, in the **Table Size** group, adjust the **Height** or **Width** setting.

Format tables

You can format the text in a table in the same ways you would format regular text. You can also easily do the following:

- Align text horizontally or vertically within a cell.
- Set the text direction.
- Set the cell margins.
- Apply Quick Styles, fills, outlines, and text effects.

In addition to formatting the text in a table, you can format the table itself in the following ways:

- Apply a ready-made table style.
- Customize the style by setting various options.
- Add shading, borders, and effects such as shadows and reflections to individual cells.

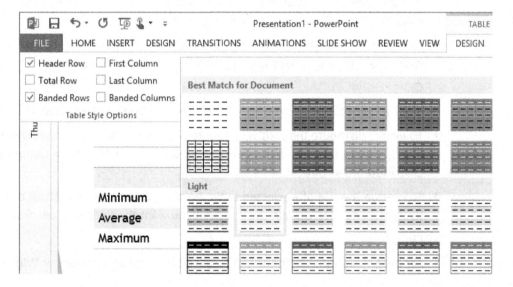

➤ **To align text**

→ On the **Layout** tool tab, in the **Alignment** group, click one of the **Align** buttons.

➤ **To set text direction**

→ In the **Alignment** group, click the **Text Direction** button, and then click one of the rotation options.

➤ **To set cell margins**

→ In the **Alignment** group, click the **Cell Margins** button, and then click one of the preset options.

→ In the **Cell Margins** list, click **Custom Margins**, and then in the **Cell Text Layout** dialog box, set specific margins.

➤ **To apply a table style**

→ On the **Design** tool tab, in the **Table Styles** gallery, click the style you want.

➤ **To format selected cells**

→ In the **Table Styles** group, click the **Shading**, **Border**, or **Effects** button, and then click the options you want.

➤ **To create a custom table style**

→ On the **Design** tool tab, in the **Table Style Options** group, select or clear the six check boxes to format the table cells to suit your data.

➤ **To apply Quick Styles and other fancy formatting**

→ On the **Design** tool tab, in the **WordArt Styles** group, click the **Quick Styles** button, and then click the style you want.

→ In the **WordArt Styles** group, click the **Text Fill**, **Text Outline**, or **Text Effects** button, and then click the options you want in the corresponding galleries.

Practice tasks

The practice files for these tasks are located in the MOSPowerPoint2013\Objective3 practice file folder. Save the results of the tasks in the same folder.

- Open the *PowerPoint_3-2a* presentation, and then perform the following tasks on slide 2:
  - ○ Insert a table that has three columns and four rows.
  - ○ In the top row of the table, enter *Task*, *Minutes/Day*, and *Hours Saved/Week*.
  - ○ Enter the following in the cells of the Task column: *Paper documents*, *Email*, and *Calendar*.
  - ○ Insert a new row at the top of the table, and merge all the cells in the row. In the merged cell, enter and center the title *Effect of Focused Activity*.
  - ○ In the table, turn off Banded Rows formatting, and turn on First Column formatting. Then apply the Medium Style 2 - Accent 2 style to the table, and apply a border around the entire table.
- On slide 3 of the *PowerPoint_3-2a* presentation, perform the following tasks:
  - ○ Embed the *PowerPoint_3-2b* worksheet.
  - ○ Enlarge the worksheet object so that it fills the available space on the slide.

3.3 Insert and format charts

Create and import charts

You can easily add a chart to a slide to help identify trends that might not be obvious from looking at numbers. When you create a chart in PowerPoint, you specify the chart type and then use a linked Excel worksheet to enter the information you want to plot. As you replace the sample data in the worksheet with your own data, you immediately see the results in the chart in the adjacent PowerPoint window.

You can enter the data directly into the linked worksheet, or you can copy and paste it from an existing Microsoft Access table, Word table, or Excel worksheet. You then identify the chart data range in the linked worksheet to ensure that only the data you want appears in the chart, and close the worksheet to plot the data.

By default, a chart is plotted based on the series of data points in the columns of the attached worksheet, and these series are identified in the legend. You can tell PowerPoint to plot the chart based on the series in the rows instead.

When a chart is active on a slide, the Design, Layout, and Format tool tabs are available on the ribbon.

At any time after you plot data in the chart, you can reopen the attached worksheet and edit the data; PowerPoint updates the chart to reflect your changes.

> **To create a chart**

1. In a content placeholder, click the **Insert Chart** button.

   Or

   On the **Insert** tab, in the **Illustrations** group, click the **Chart** button.

2. In the **Insert Chart** dialog box, click a chart category in the left pane, click a chart type in the right pane, and then click **OK**.

3. In the linked Excel worksheet, enter the values to be plotted, following the pattern of the sample data.

4. Ensure that the blue border delineating the chart data range encompasses only the data you want included in the chart, by dragging the blue handle in the lower-right corner of the range.

5. Close the Excel window.

> **To insert a chart from Excel**

1. In the source workbook, click the chart border to select it.

2. Copy the chart to the Clipboard.

3. Switch to PowerPoint, display the slide, and then paste the chart from the Clipboard.

> **To open the attached worksheet so that you can edit the chart data**

→ Right-click the chart, and then click **Edit Data**.

→ Click the chart, and then on the **Design** tool tab, in the **Data** group, click the **Edit Data** button.

> **Tip** The chart must be active (surrounded by a frame) when you make changes to the data in the worksheet; otherwise, the chart won't automatically update.

> **To plot a selected chart by rows instead of columns**

1. Open the chart's attached worksheet.

2. On the **Design** tool tab, in the **Data** group, click the **Switch Row/Column** button.

> **Tip** The Switch Row/Column button is active only when the worksheet is open.

> **To select worksheet data for editing**

→ To select a cell, click it.

→ To select a column, click the column header (the letter at the top of the column).

→ To select a row, click the row header (the number at the left end of the row).

→ To select multiple cells, columns, or rows, select the first element, and then hold down the **Shift** key as you select subsequent elements.

Or

Drag through adjacent cells, columns, or rows.

→ To select an entire worksheet, click the **Select All** button (the triangle in the upper-left corner of the worksheet, at the intersection of the row and column headers).

Change the chart type, layout, and elements

If you decide that the type of chart you initially selected doesn't adequately depict your data, you can change the type at any time. There are 10 chart categories, each with two-dimensional and three-dimensional variations.

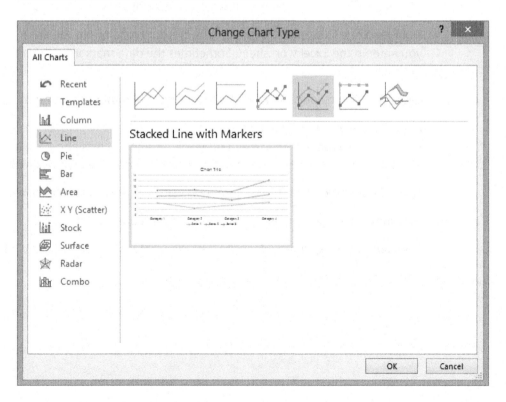

Each chart type has corresponding chart layouts that you can use to refine the look of the chart.

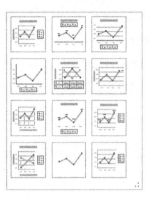

These layouts are preset combinations of the available chart elements, which include the following:

- **Chart area** This is the entire area within the chart frame.

- **Plot area** This is the rectangle between the horizontal and vertical axes.

- **Data markers** These are the graphical representations of the values, or *data points*, you enter in the Excel worksheet. Sometimes the data markers are identified with data labels.

- **Legend** This provides a key for identifying the *data series* (a set of data points).

- **Axes** The data is plotted against an x-axis—also called the category axis—and a y-axis—also called the *value axis*. (Three-dimensional charts also have a z-axis—also called the *series axis*.) Sometimes the axes are identified with axis labels.

- **Axis labels** These identify the categories, values, or series along each axis.

- **Gridlines** These help to visually quantify the data points.

- **Data table** This table provides details of the plotted data points in table format.

- **Titles** The chart might have a title and subtitle.

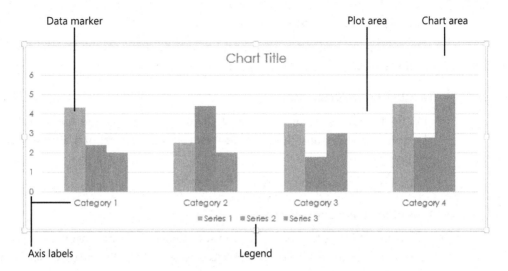

When the preset layouts don't produce the chart you want, you can create a custom layout by mixing and matching different chart elements.

You can adjust a chart layout by adding, deleting, moving, and sizing chart elements. To perform any of those tasks, you must first select the element.

If you want more control over the layout of a chart, you can do the following:

- Control the overall size of the chart.
- Adjust the size of chart elements.
- Arrange chart elements precisely.

➤ **To change the type of a selected chart**

1. On the **Design** tool tab, in the **Type** group, click the **Change Chart Type** button.
2. In the **Change Chart Type** dialog box, click a category on the left, click a chart type at the top, and then click **OK**.

> **Tip** Click a chart type in the top row to preview that chart type as applied to the current data. Point to the preview to display a larger version.

➤ **To apply a preset layout to a selected chart**

→ On the **Design** tool tab, in the **Chart Layouts** gallery, click the **Quick Layout** button, and then click the layout you want.

➤ **To add or remove an axis**

→ On the **Design** tool tab, in the **Chart Layouts** group, click the **Add Chart Element** button, click **Axes**, and then click to select **Primary Horizontal**, **Primary Vertical**, or both.

→ Click a selected axis to remove it from the chart.

➤ **To add or remove an axis title**

→ In the **Chart Layouts** group, click the **Add Chart Element** button, click **Axis Titles**, and then click to select **Primary Horizontal Axis Title**, **Primary Vertical Axis Title**, or both.

→ Click a selected axis title to remove it from the chart.

➤ **To add or remove a chart title**

→ In the **Chart Layouts** group, click the **Add Chart Element** button, click **Chart Title**, and then click **None**, **Above Chart**, or **Centered Overlay**.

➤ **To add or remove data labels**

→ In the **Chart Layouts** group, click the **Add Chart Element** button, click **Data Labels**, and then click **None**, **Center**, **Inside End**, **Inside Base**, **Outside End**, or **Data Callout**.

➤ **To add or remove a data table**

→ In the **Chart Layouts** group, click the **Add Chart Element** button, click **Data Table**, and then click **None**, **With Legend Keys**, or **No Legend Keys**.

➤ **To add or remove error bars**

→ In the **Chart Layouts** group, click the **Add Chart Element** button, click **Legend**, and then click **None**, **Standard Error**, **Percentage**, or **Deviation**.

➤ **To add or remove gridlines**

→ In the **Chart Layouts** group, click the **Add Chart Element** button, click **Gridlines**, and then click to select **Primary Major Horizontal**, **Primary Major Vertical**, **Primary Minor Horizontal**, **Primary Minor Vertical**, or any combination of the four options.

→ Click a selected gridline option to remove it from the chart.

➤ **To add or remove a legend**

➜ In the **Chart Layouts** group, click the **Add Chart Element** button, click **Legend**, and then click **None**, **Right**, **Top**, **Left**, or **Bottom**.

➤ **To add or remove lines (line charts only)**

➜ In the **Chart Layouts** group, click the **Add Chart Element** button, click **Lines**, and then click **None**, **Drop Lines**, or **High-Low Lines**.

➤ **To add or remove a trendline (line charts only)**

➜ In the **Chart Layouts** group, click the **Add Chart Element** button, click **Trendline**, and then click **None**, **Linear**, **Exponential**, **Linear Forecast**, or **Moving Average**.

> **Tip** You can use standard techniques to add pictures, shapes, and independent text boxes to slides to enhance charts.

➤ **To change the size of a selected chart**

➜ Point to any handle (the sets of dots around the chart frame), and when the hollow double-headed arrow appears, drag in the direction you want the chart to grow or shrink.

➤ **To select a chart element**

➜ Click the element once.

➜ If the element is difficult to identify or click, on the **Format** tool tab, in the **Current Selection** group, display the **Chart Elements** list, and then click the element you want.

> **Tip** If you want to activate the chart (that is, select the chart area), be sure to click a blank area inside the chart frame. Clicking any of the chart's elements will activate that element, not the chart as a whole.

➤ **To change the size of a selected chart element**

➜ Point to any handle, and when the hollow double-headed arrow appears, drag in the direction you want the element to grow or shrink.

> **Tip** If an element cannot be sized, the hollow double-headed arrow does not appear.

➤ **To change the position of a selected chart element**

→ Point to the border around the element, away from any handles, and when the four-headed arrow appears, drag to the desired position.

> **Tip** Some elements cannot be moved, even if the four-headed arrow appears.

➤ **To rotate a three-dimensional chart layout**

1. Right-click the chart, and then click **3-D Rotation**.

2. In the **3-D Rotation** area of the **Effects** page of the **Format Chart Area** pane, set the angle of rotation for each axis.

Format charts

You can modify and format a chart to get the effect you want. If you don't want to spend a lot of time on individual chart elements, you can apply styles (predefined combinations of formatting) to the chart area (the entire chart) to create sophisticated charts with a minimum of effort. These styles include the following:

- **Chart styles** Combinations of data marker, wall, and floor fill colors, background color, and bevel effects

- **Shape styles** Combinations of shape fills, shape outlines, and shape effects

- **WordArt styles** Combinations of text fills, text outlines, and text effects

You can also apply shape style and WordArt style components individually, both to the chart area and to a selected chart element.

In addition to using styles and style components, you can fine-tune the formatting of a selected chart element in its Format pane.

Each type of element has a specific Format pane. Most panes have multiple pages presenting options such as the following:

- **Chart area** You can specify the background fill, the border color and style, effects such as shadows and edges, the 3-D format and rotation, and the size and position. You can also attach text to be displayed when someone points to the chart.

- **Plot area** You can specify the background fill, the border color and style, effects such as shadows and edges, and the 3-D format and rotation.

- **Data markers** You can specify the background fill, the border color and style, effects such as shadows and edges, and the 3-D format. You can also precisely determine the gap between data points.

- **Legend** You can specify the background fill, the border color and style, and effects such as shadows and edges. You can also specify the legend's position and whether it can overlap the chart.

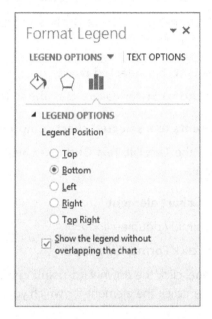

- **Axes** You can specify the background fill, the line color and style, effects such as shadows and edges, and the 3-D format and rotation. For the category axis, you can also specify the scale, add or remove tick marks, adjust the label position, and determine the starting and maximum values. You can set the number format (such as currency or percentage), and set the axis label alignment.

- **Gridlines** You can set the line color, line style, and effects such as shadows and edges.

- **Data table** You can specify the background fill, the border color and style, effects such as shadows and edges, and the 3-D format. You can also set table borders.

- **Titles** You can specify the background fill, the border color and style, effects such as shadows and edges, and the 3-D format. You can also set the title's alignment, direction, and angle of rotation.

➤ **To apply a chart style to a selected chart**

→ On the **Design** tool tab, in the **Chart Styles** gallery, click the style you want.

➤ **To apply a shape style to a selected chart component**

→ On the **Format** tool tab, in the **Shape Styles** gallery, click the style you want.

➤ **To apply shape style components to a selected chart component**

→ In the **Shape Styles** group, click the **Shape Fill**, **Shape Outline**, or **Shape Effects** button, and then click the option you want.

➤ **To apply a WordArt style to the text in a selected chart**

→ On the **Format** tool tab, in the **WordArt Styles** gallery, click the style you want.

➤ **To apply WordArt style components to a selected chart component**

→ In the **WordArt Styles** group, click the **Text Fill**, **Text Outline**, or **Text Effects** button, and then click the option you want.

➤ **To display the Format pane for a chart element**

→ If the element is easy to identify, simply double-click it.

→ Right-click the element, and then click **Format** *Element*.

→ At the top of an open **Format** pane, click the downward-pointing triangle to the right of the **Options** label, and then click the element for which you want to display the Format pane.

Or

1. If you have trouble double-clicking a smaller chart element, on the **Format** tool tab, in the **Current Selection** group, display the **Chart Elements** list, and then click the element you want.

2. In the **Current Selection** group, click the **Format Selection** button.

> **Tip** To display the Format Major Gridlines pane, right-click any gridline, and then click Format Gridlines. To display the Format Data Table pane, right-click the selected data table, and then click Format Data Table.

Practice tasks

The practice files for these tasks are located in the MOSPowerPoint2013\Objective3 practice file folder. Save the results of the tasks in the same folder.

- Open the *PowerPoint_3-3a* presentation. On slide 2, use the data from cells A3:C9 of the *PowerPoint_3-3b* workbook to create a Clustered Column chart.

- In the chart on slide 2, perform the following tasks:
  - Change the Average data point for Brushing Teeth to *4* and the Conservative data point to *2*.
  - Change the chart type to Stacked Line With Markers.
  - Apply Quick Layout 3.

- On slide 3, change the way the data is plotted so that the columns are clustered by month and the legend identifies the Minimum, Average, and Maximum series.

- Open the *PowerPoint_3-3c* presentation, and then perform the following tasks on slide 3:
  - Apply Style 7 to the entire chart. Then, with the entire chart still selected, apply the Moderate Effect – Tan, Accent 2 shape style.
  - Apply the Fill – White, Outline – Accent 1, Glow – Accent 1 WordArt style to the chart title.
  - Explode the data points in the chart by 20 percent, and then set the angle of the first slice at 200.
  - Move the chart legend to the right, and then fill its background with the Gray-50%, Accent 6, Darker 25% color.

3.4 Insert and format SmartArt

Insert and modify SmartArt graphics

When you want to clearly illustrate a concept such as a process, cycle, hierarchy, or relationship, the powerful SmartArt Graphics tool makes it easy to create dynamic, visually appealing diagrams. The content of the diagram is controlled by a single-level or multiple-level list. The appearance is controlled by the SmartArt template. By using the available templates, you can easily construct any of the following types of diagrams:

- **List** These diagrams visually represent lists of related or independent information—for example, a list of items needed to complete a task, including pictures of the items.

- **Process** These diagrams visually describe the ordered set of steps required to complete a task—for example, the steps for getting a project approved.

- **Cycle** These diagrams represent a circular sequence of steps, tasks, or events, or the relationship of a set of steps, tasks, or events to a central, core element—for example, the looping process for continually improving a product based on customer feedback.

- **Hierarchy** These diagrams illustrate the structure of an organization or entity—for example, the top-level management structure of a company.

- **Relationship** These diagrams show convergent, divergent, overlapping, merging, or containment elements—for example, how using similar methods to organize your email, calendar, and contacts can improve your productivity.

- **Matrix** These diagrams show the relationship of components to a whole—for example, the product teams in a department.

- **Pyramid** These diagrams illustrate proportional or interconnected relationships—for example, the amount of time that should ideally be spent on different phases of a project.

- **Picture** These diagrams rely on pictures in addition to text to create one of the other types of diagrams—for example, a process picture diagram with photographs showing the recession of glaciers in Glacier National Park. Picture diagrams are a subset of the other categories but are also available from their own category so that you can easily locate diagram layouts that support images.

SmartArt graphic layouts are available from the Choose A SmartArt Graphic dialog box. The categories are not mutually exclusive, meaning that some layouts appear in more than one category. PowerPoint 2013 includes some new built-in SmartArt templates, and an internal connection to additional templates on the Office website.

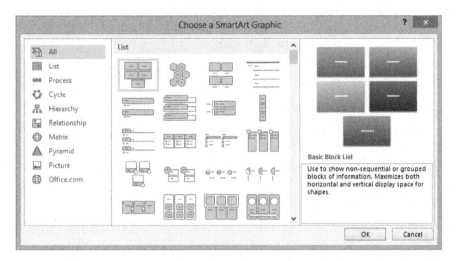

After you choose a layout, PowerPoint inserts the basic diagram into the slide and displays the associated list format in the Text pane, into which you can enter information. (If the Text pane doesn't open automatically, you can display it by clicking the button on the left edge of the diagram.) You can enter more or less information than is depicted by the original diagram; most diagrams support a range of entries (although a few are formatted to support only a specific number of entries). You can insert and modify text either directly in the diagram shapes or in the associated Text pane. The selected layout determines whether the text appears in or adjacent to its shapes.

> **Tip** You change the size, shape, and location of a SmartArt graphic by using the same techniques you use with other graphic elements.

After you create a diagram and add the text you want to display in it, you might find that the diagram layout you originally selected doesn't precisely meet your needs. You can easily change to a different diagram layout without losing any of the information you entered in the diagram. If a particular layout doesn't support the amount or level of information that is associated with the diagram, the extra text will be hidden but not deleted, and will be available when you choose another layout that supports it.

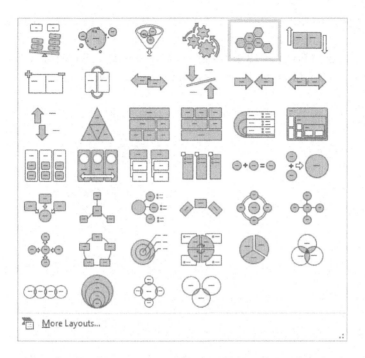

> **Tip** If a gallery has a sizing handle (three dots) in its lower-right corner, you can resize it. By reducing the height of the gallery, you can display more of the slide and the gallery at the same time.

When you decide on the layout you want to use, you can add and remove shapes and edit the text of the diagram either by making changes in the Text pane or by using the options on the SmartArt tool tabs.

You can make changes such as the following by using the commands on the Design tool tab:

- Add shading and three-dimensional effects to all the shapes in a diagram.
- Change the color scheme.
- Add shapes and change their hierarchy.
- Reverse the order of shapes.

> **Tip** You can rearrange shapes by dragging them.

You can customize individual shapes in the following ways:

- Change an individual shape—for example, change a square into a star.
- Apply a built-in shape style.
- Change the color, outline, or effect of a shape.
- Change the style of the shape's text.

The Live Preview feature displays the effects of these changes before you apply them. If you apply changes and then decide you preferred the original version, you can easily click the return to the unaltered diagram layout.

In PowerPoint (but not in other Office programs), you can easily convert an ordinary bulleted list to a SmartArt graphic that retains the relationship of the bullet levels. Or you can create the diagram and then add text, either directly to its shapes or as a bulleted list in the Text pane, which opens to the left of the diagram. In the Text pane, you can add shapes, delete shapes, and rearrange them by dragging the associated list items.

➤ **To create a SmartArt diagram from a bulleted list**

➜ Right-click any item in the list, click **Convert to SmartArt**, and then click the layout you want.

➜ Right-click any item in the list, click **More SmartArt Graphics**, click a layout in the **Choose SmartArt Graphic** dialog box, and then click **OK**.

➤ **To create an empty SmartArt graphic**

1. On the **Insert** tab, in the **Illustrations** group, click the **SmartArt** button.
2. In the left pane of the **Choose a SmartArt Graphic** dialog box, click the type of diagram you want.
3. In the center pane, click the layout you want, and then click **OK**.

➤ **To add text to a SmartArt diagram**

➜ Click a shape, and then enter the text.

   Or

1. Open the **Text** pane by doing one of the following:
   - ○ Click the button (labeled with a left-pointing chevron) on the left side of the diagram's frame.
   - ○ On the **Design** tool tab, in the **Create Graphic** group, click the **Text Pane** button.
2. Replace the placeholder list items with your own text.

➤ **To add a shape**

→ In the **Text** pane, at the right end of the bullet after which you want to add the shape, press **Enter**, and then enter the text for the new shape.

→ Click the shape after which you want to add the shape, and then on the **Design** tool tab, in the **Create Graphic** group, click the **Add Shape** button.

> **Tip** To add a shape before the selected shape, display the Add Shape list, and then click Add Shape Before.

➤ **To promote or demote a first-level diagram shape to a subordinate entry**

→ On the **Design** tool tab, in the **Create Graphic** group, click the **Promote** or **Demote** button.

→ In the **Text** pane, click at the left end of an entry, and then press **Tab** to demote it or **Shift+Tab** to promote it.

> **Tip** Some SmartArt diagrams are not formatted to accept subordinate entries.

➤ **To move an existing shape**

→ On the **Design** tool tab, in the **Create Graphic** group, click the **Move Up** or **Move Down** button.

➤ **To reverse the order of shapes in a SmartArt graphic**

→ On the **Design** tool tab, in the **Create Graphic** group, click the **Right To Left** button.

➤ **To delete a shape from a SmartArt graphic**

→ In the diagram, click the shape, and then press the **Delete** key.

→ In the **Text** pane, select the list item, and then press the **Delete** key.

➤ **To change the color scheme of a selected diagram**

→ On the **Design** tool tab, in the **SmartArt Styles** group, click the **Change Colors** button, and then click the color scheme you want.

➤ **To apply a style to a selected diagram**

→ On the **Design** tool tab, in the **SmartArt Styles** gallery, click the style you want to apply.

➤ **To apply a style to a selected diagram shape**

→ On the **Format** tool tab, in the **Shape Styles** gallery, click the style you want to apply.

Or

1. On the **Format** tool tab, click the **Shape Styles** dialog box launcher.
2. In the **Format Shape** pane, on the **Fill & Line**, **Effects**, and **Layout & Properties** pages, choose the effects you want to apply.

➤ **To reset diagram modifications**

→ On the **Design** tool tab, in the **Reset** group, click the **Reset Graphic** button.

> **Strategy** Many formatting options are available from the Design and Format tool tabs. Be familiar with the options available on the tool tabs and in the associated dialog boxes.

Practice tasks

The practice file for these tasks is located in the MOSPowerPoint2013\Objective3 practice file folder. Save the results of the tasks in the same folder.

- Open the *PowerPoint_3-4* presentation, and then perform the following tasks:
    - On slide 3, insert an Organization Chart SmartArt graphic and use the names of people you know to diagram an organization that includes one manager with one assistant and three employees.
    - Delete the manager's assistant from the organization chart, and then add an assistant for one of the employees.
    - On slide 4, convert the bulleted list to a Continuous Block Process diagram. Then change the layout to Basic Venn.
    - On slide 4, change the style of the diagram to 3-D Polished, and change the colors to Colorful – Accent Colors. Then format the text as Fill – White, Drop Shadow. Finally, change the color of the Administration & Human Resources shape to Dark Red.

3.5 Insert and format images

Insert images

You can insert digital photographs or pictures created in almost any program into a PowerPoint presentation. Office 2013 applications classify images in these two categories:

- **Pictures** Pictures that are saved as files on your computer, on a network drive, or on a device (such as a digital camera) that is connected to your computer

- **Online Pictures** Royalty-free clip art images from Office.com, web search results from Bing, or images stored in your personal online storage folder

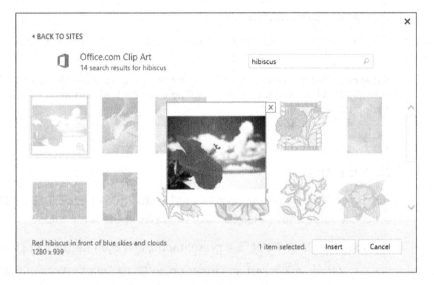

You can also capture and insert images of content displayed on your computer screen directly from PowerPoint. By using the built-in screen clipping tool, you can insert screen captures of entire windows or selected areas of on-screen content.

> **Strategy** Capturing and inserting images by using the screen clipping tool is beyond the scope of MOS Exam 77-422: Microsoft PowerPoint 2013.

➤ **To insert an image from a file**

1. In a content placeholder, or in the **Images** group on the **Insert** tab, click the **Pictures** button.

2. In the **Insert Picture** dialog box, browse to and click the file you want. Then do one of the following:

   ○ Click **Insert** to insert the image on the slide.

   ○ In the **Insert** list, click **Link to File** to insert an image that will update automatically if the image file changes.

   ○ In the **Insert** list, click **Insert and Link** to insert an image that you can manually update if the image file changes.

➤ **To insert an online image**

1. In a content placeholder, or in the **Images** group on the **Insert** tab, click the **Online Pictures** button.

2. In the **Insert Pictures** window, click the online source (Office.com, Bing Image Search, a SharePoint site or online storage folder, or one of the available linked third-party sites).

3. Enter a keyword in the search box and then press **Enter**, or browse to the picture you want to insert.

4. Double-click the image you want to insert.

> **Tip** You change the size, shape, layout, and location of images by using the same techniques that you use with other graphic elements and in other Office 2013 programs.

Format images

After you insert an image on a slide, you can modify it in many ways. For example, you can crop or resize an image, change the image's brightness and contrast, recolor it, and apply artistic effects to it. You can apply a wide range of preformatted styles to an image to change its shape and orientation, and also to add borders and picture effects.

You modify the image by using commands on the Format tool tab, which is displayed only when an object is selected.

- The Adjust group contains commands that enable you to change the image's brightness and contrast, recolor it, apply artistic effects to it, and compress it to reduce the size of the presentation.

- The Picture Styles group offers a wide range of picture styles that you can apply to an image to change its shape and orientation, and to add borders and picture effects. This group includes the Quick Styles gallery, which contains many style combinations that you can apply very quickly.

- The Arrange group contains commands for specifying the relationship of the image to the page and to other elements on the page.

- The Size group contains commands for cropping and resizing images.

➤ **To apply a style to a selected image**

→ On the **Format** tool tab, in the **Picture Styles** group, expand the **Quick Styles** gallery, and then click the style you want to apply.

Or

1. On the **Format** tool tab, click the **Picture Styles** dialog box launcher.

2. In the **Format Picture** pane, on the **Fill & Line**, **Effects**, **Layout & Properties**, and **Picture** pages, choose the settings you want to apply, and then click **Close**.

➤ **To apply artistic effects to a selected image**

➜ On the **Format** tool tab, in the **Adjust** group, expand the **Artistic Effects** gallery, and then click the effect you want to apply.

➤ **To apply picture effects to a selected image**

➜ On the **Format** tool tab, in the **Picture Styles** group, click **Picture Effects**, point to any category to expand the gallery, and then click the effect you want to apply.

➤ **To change the brightness, contrast, or color of a selected image**

➜ In the **Format Picture** pane, on the **Picture** page, modify the settings in the **Picture Corrections** and **Picture Color** sections.

➤ **To change the size or shape of a selected image**

➜ Drag its sizing handles.

➜ On the **Format** tool tab, in the **Size** group, change the **Shape Height** and **Shape Width** settings.

➜ On the **Format** tool tab, click the **Size** dialog box launcher. Then on the **Size & Properties** page of the **Format Picture** pane, change the **Height**, **Width**, or **Scale** settings.

Practice tasks

The practice file for these tasks is located in the MOSPowerPoint2013\Objective3 practice file folder. Save the results of the tasks in the same folder.

- Open the *PowerPoint_3-5* presentation, and then perform the following tasks:
    - ○ On slide 4, insert an image from the Office.com Clip Art gallery that depicts someone skiing.
    - ○ Set the height of the image to 3" and position the image in the lower-right corner of the slide.
    - ○ If appropriate, remove the background from the image to isolate the skier.
    - ○ Preview the available picture styles and apply the one that most suits the image.
    - ○ Recolor the image so that it matches the slide color scheme.

3.6 Insert and format media

Embed audio and video clips

There are many ways of communicating information to audiences. PowerPoint is primarily a visual medium through which a presenter displays static information. However, PowerPoint presentations can also include sound and video.

In addition to the sound effects that are available for slide transitions, you can play audio clips for a specific length of time or throughout an entire slide show. For example, you might include light background music during a slide show that plays repeatedly while an audience is entering the room, emphasize a point by playing a sound clip, or prerecord the audio presentation for each slide. You can insert audio clips from an online or local source, or record them directly in PowerPoint.

The Office.com Clip Art gallery includes royalty-free sound clips of many kinds, including sound effects and music.

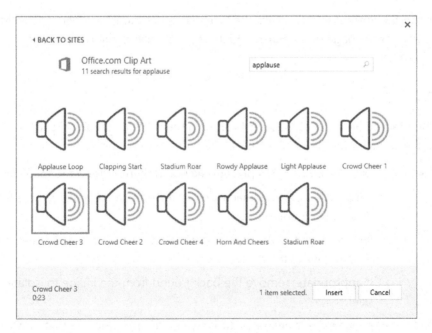

If part of the information that you want to convey to your audience is in video form, you can embed that video on a slide instead of having to play it from a different device. This helps to keep your audience focused on your presentation, and simplifies the setup necessary to present the video. You can insert video clips from an online or local source.

The available online sources include only those that require corporate credentials or a Microsoft account, to ensure that private videos aren't used without permission.

> **Tip** If you want to link to a video stored on YouTube or a similar online service, you can generate links from within that service to include on slides.

➤ **To insert a local audio clip**

1. On the **Insert** tab, in the **Media** group, click the **Audio** button, and then click **Audio on My PC**.

2. In the **Insert Audio** window, browse to the audio file location, click the audio file or thumbnail, and then click **Insert**.

➤ **To insert an online audio clip**

1. On the **Insert** tab, in the **Media** group, click the **Audio** button, and then click **Online Audio**.

2. In the **Insert Audio** window, click the audio source, browse to the audio file location, click the audio file or thumbnail, and then click **Insert**.

   Or

   In the **Insert Audio** window, click **Office.com Clip Art**, enter a search term in the search box, and then press **Enter**. In the search results, click the sound icon for the audio clip you want to use, and then click **Insert**.

> **Tip** When you point to or click an audio clip icon, the name and length of the audio clip appear in the lower-left corner of the window, and the audio clip plays.

➤ **To record and embed an audio clip**

1. On the **Insert** tab, in the **Media** group, click the **Audio** button, and then click **Record Audio**.

2. In the **Record Sound** window, enter a name for the audio clip, and then click the **Record** button (the red dot).

3. Deliver the audio content that you want to record, and when you finish, click the **Stop** button (the blue square). Then click **OK** to embed the recorded audio on the slide.

➤ **To insert a local video clip**

1. In a content placeholder, click the **Insert Video** button. Then in the **Insert Video** window, click **From a file**.

   Or

   On the **Insert** tab, in the **Media** group, click the **Video** button, and then click **Video on My PC**.

2. In the **Insert Video** window, browse to the video location, click the video file or thumbnail, and click **Insert**.

➤ **To insert an online video clip**

1. In a content placeholder, click the **Insert Video** button.

   Or

   On the **Insert** tab, in the **Media** group, click the **Video** button, and then click **Online Video**.

2. In the **Insert Video** window, click the video source. Then browse to the video location, click the video file or thumbnail, and click **Insert**.

> **Tip** To preview a video from an online source, point to the video thumbnail and click the View Larger button that appears in the lower-right corner of the thumbnail. To close the preview window, click the Close button (the X) in the upper-right corner of the window.

Modify audio and video clips

When you insert an audio clip on a slide, a speaker icon appears in the center of the slide. You can move or resize the icon, and hide it during a slide show. When the speaker icon is selected, PowerPoint displays a Play/Pause button, a progress bar, an elapsed time counter, and a volume control. You can configure audio to play automatically, to play for a specific amount of time, or to loop continuously during a specific slide or the entire presentation. You can fade gradually into and out of an audio clip. You can also trim the audio clip to play only a specific portion of it.

After you insert a video clip, you can resize the window it appears in, or even crop the area of the video that is displayed. By default, a video clip plays within its window, but you can configure it to play at full-screen size. You can also configure most of the same playback options for video clips that you can for audio clips.

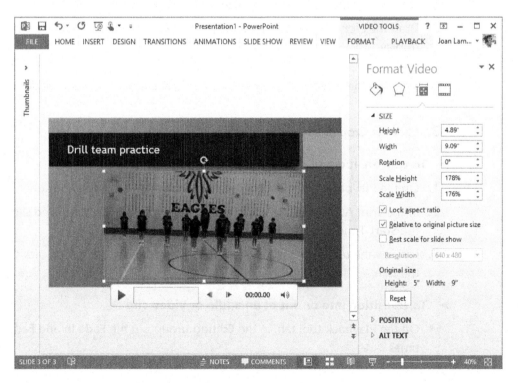

It isn't necessary to edit audio or video prior to inserting it in a presentation. You can trim audio and video clips in much the same way that you can format the appearance of a picture: although the audience hears or sees only what you select, the original media is unaltered.

➤ **To modify the appearance of a selected audio icon or video window**

→ On the **Format** tool tab, in the **Adjust**, **Picture Styles**, or **Video Styles** group, configure the formatting options you want.

➤ **To resize a video window**

→ Drag the window sizing handles.

→ On the **Format** tool tab, in the **Size** group, set the **Video Height** or **Video Width**, and then press **Enter**.

→ On the **Format** tool tab, click the **Size** dialog box launcher. In the **Format Video** pane, configure the height, width, rotation, scale, and aspect ratio settings.

➤ **To crop a video window**

1. On the **Format** tool tab, in the **Size** group, click the **Crop** button.

2. Drag the crop handles to frame the portion of the video window that you want to display.

> **Tip** Drag the crop frame to move it to a different part of the video window.

3. Click the **Crop** button again to apply the changes.

➤ **To trim an audio or video clip**

1. On the **Playback** tool tab, click the **Trim Audio** or **Trim Video** button.

2. In the **Trim Audio** or **Trim Video** dialog box, drag the **Start** and **End** sliders, or set the **Start Time** and **End Time**.

3. Preview the results and make adjustments as necessary, and then click **OK** to apply the trim.

➤ **To transition into or out of an audio or video clip**

→ On the **Playback** tool tab, in the **Editing** group, set the **Fade In** and **Fade Out** times.

➤ **To configure the playback options for an audio clip**

→ On the **Playback** tool tab, in the **Audio Options** group, do any of the following:

○ Click **Volume**, and then click **Low**, **Medium**, **High**, or **Mute**.

○ In the **Start** list, click **On Click** or **Automatically**.

○ Select the **Play Across Slides** check box to continue playing the clip when the next slide is displayed.

○ Select the **Loop until Stopped** check box to automatically restart the clip when it ends.

○ Select the **Hide During Show** check box to hide the audio icon when the slide is shown.

○ Select the **Rewind after Playing** check box to automatically return to the beginning of the clip when it finishes.

→ On the **Playback** tool tab, in the **Audio Styles** group, click the **Play in Background** button to set the audio options necessary to play the clip continuously from the slide on which it starts until the presentation ends or the clip is stopped.

➤ **To configure the playback options for a video clip**

→ On the **Playback** tool tab, in the **Video Options** group, do any of the following:

○ Click **Volume**, and then click **Low**, **Medium**, **High**, or **Mute**.

○ In the **Start** list, click **On Click** or **Automatically**.

○ Select the **Play Full Screen** check box to expand the video to full-screen size while it is playing.

○ Select the **Hide While Not Playing** check box to hide the video window after the video ends.

○ Select the **Loop until Stopped** check box to automatically restart the clip when it ends.

○ Select the **Rewind after Playing** check box to automatically return to the beginning of the clip when it finishes.

Practice tasks

The practice files for these tasks are located in the MOSPowerPoint2013\Objective3 practice file folder. Save the results of the tasks in the same folder.

- Open the *PowerPoint_3-6a* presentation and perform the following tasks:
  - ○ On slide 1, insert the audio clip named Caribbean Dance 1 from the Office.com Clip Art gallery.
  - ○ On the Playback tool tab, in the Audio Styles group, select all the options necessary to configure the audio clip as a soundtrack to the presentation.
  - ○ On slide 2, insert the *PowerPoint_3-6b* video clip. The video clip is 2 minutes, 40 seconds in length.
  - ○ Trim the video to 1 minute, starting 25 seconds into the original clip.
  - ○ Configure the video to start automatically when the slide appears, and to fade out at the end.
  - ○ Mute the sound of the video so that it does not compete with the Caribbean soundtrack.
  - ○ Adjust the video to the size at which you'd like to display it, and then center it in the slide content pane.
  - ○ Test the soundtrack and video by playing the slide show.
  - ○ Save and close the presentation.

Objective review

Before finishing this chapter, ensure that you have mastered the following skills:

3.1 Insert and format text

3.2 Insert and format tables

3.3 Insert and format charts

3.4 Insert and format SmartArt

3.5 Insert and format images

3.6 Insert and format media

4 Apply transitions and animations

The skills tested in this section of the Microsoft Office Specialist exam for Microsoft PowerPoint 2013 relate to applying transitions and animations. Specifically, the following objectives are associated with this set of skills:

4.1 Apply transitioning between slides

4.2 Animate slide content

4.3 Set timing for transitions and animations

When you deliver a presentation, you can move from slide to slide by clicking the mouse button, or you can have PowerPoint replace one slide with the next at predetermined intervals. One of the ways in which you can keep an audience's attention is by applying an interesting transition effect when moving between slides. Another way to keep the audience's interest, and often to communicate additional information, is to animate text and objects on slides. By incorporating dynamic effects, you can emphasize key points, control the focus of the discussion, and entertain in ways that will make your message memorable.

This chapter guides you in studying ways of configuring slide transitions and animating slide content.

> **Practice Files** To complete the practice tasks in this chapter, you need the practice files contained in the MOSPowerPoint2013\Objective4 practice file folder. For more information, see "Download the practice files" in this book's Introduction.

4.1 Apply transitioning between slides

Transitions control the way slides move into and out of view during a slide show. They include simple effects such as sliding in, more complex effects such as dissolving in from the outer edges or the center, and very fancy effects such as scattering the slide content like glitter.

All the base transition effects are available in the Transitions gallery. The transition effects are divided into three categories: Subtle, Exciting, and Dynamic Content.

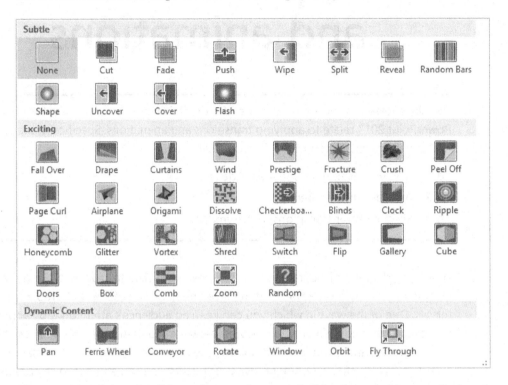

The transition from one slide to the next is controlled by the transition applied to the incoming slide. Each slide can have only one transition effect. You can set transitions in Normal view or Slide Sorter view. You can set a transition for one slide, for a group of slides, or for an entire presentation.

Depending on the type of transition, you might be able to further refine its effect by clicking a specific option on the related Effect Options menu.

In addition to any available effect options, you can specify the following:

- An associated sound
- The transition speed
- When the transition occurs

> **See Also** For information about transition speed and triggers, see section 4.3, "Set timing for transitions and animations."

As with all effects, be careful not to overdo it. Consider the tone and purpose of a presentation when applying transitions.

➤ **To apply a transition to a selected slide or slides**

→ On the **Transitions** tab, in the **Transition to This Slide** group, display the **Transitions** gallery, and then click the transition you want.

➤ **To modify transition effect options**

→ In the **Transition to This Slide** group, click the **Effect Options** button, and then click the effect you want.

➤ **To incorporate a sound into the transition of a selected slide**

→ On the **Transitions** tab, in the **Timing** group, display the **Sound** list, and then click the sound you want.

→ In the **Timing** group, in the **Sound** list, click **Other Sound**. In the **Add Audio** dialog box, locate and select the sound file you want to use, and then click **Open**.

➤ **To apply the transition of the selected slide to all the slides**

→ In the **Timing** group, click the **Apply To All** button.

➤ **To remove transitions between slides**

1. On the **Transitions** tab, in the **Transition to This Slide** group, display the **Transitions** gallery, and click **None**.

2. In the **Timing** group, click the **Apply To All** button.

Practice tasks

The practice files for these tasks are located in the MOSPowerPoint2013\Objective4 practice file folder. Save the results of the tasks in the same folder.

- Open the *PowerPoint_4-1a* presentation, and then complete the following tasks:
  - ○ Apply the Cover transition to all the slides in the presentation.
  - ○ Make the transition rotate from the bottom.
  - ○ Add the Wind sound to the transition, and then set the transition speed to 3 seconds.
- Open the *PowerPoint_4-1b* presentation, and remove the transition effects from all the slides.

4.2 Animate slide content

If you are delivering a presentation from your computer, you can keep your audience focused and reinforce your message by animating slide elements such as text and graphics.

Apply animations

Many common animations are available from the Animation gallery. These animations fall into four categories depending on their purpose:

- **Entrance** Animate the appearance (arrival) of an element on the slide.
- **Emphasis** Draw attention to an element by changing its size or appearance, or by making it move.
- **Exit** Animate the departure of an element from the slide.
- **Motion Paths** Move an element from one location on the slide to another, along a specific path.

> **Tip** Each Entrance effect has a corresponding Exit effect.

You can access additional animations in each category by clicking the More commands at the bottom of the Animation menu. Entrance, Emphasis, and Exit effects are classified in subcategories of Basic, Subtle, Moderate, and Exciting to help you match the effects with the tone of your presentation.

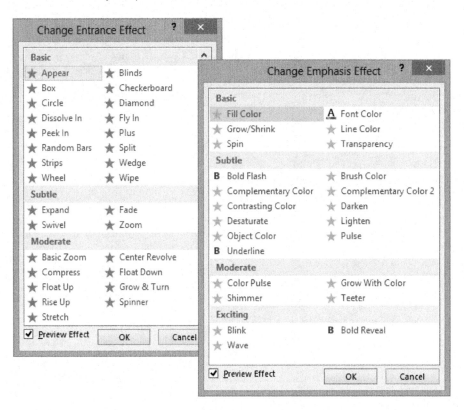

Motion Path effects are classified in subcategories of Basic, Lines & Curves, and Special to reflect the type and direction of movement in the motion path.

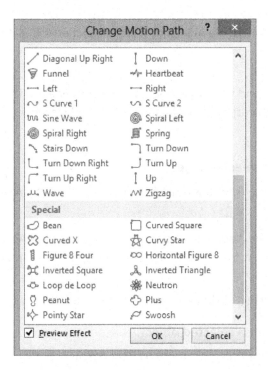

You can apply multiple animation effects to an object. On the slide and in the Animation pane, each animation is identified by an adjacent numbered box that indicates the order in which the animations will occur.

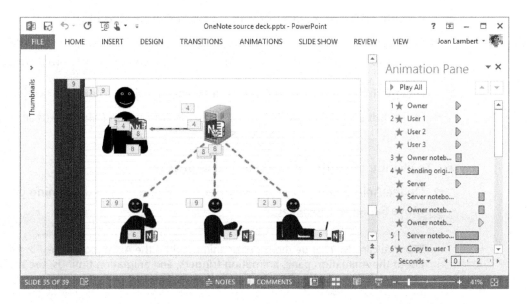

> **See Also** For more information about the Animation pane, see section 4.3, "Set timing for transitions and animations."

If you combine animation effects and want to apply the same combination to another object, you can copy the effects by using the Animation Painter, which works the same way as the Format Painter.

➤ **To apply an animation to a selected object**

→ On the **Animations** tab, in the **Animation** gallery, click the animation you want.

Or

1. On the **Animations** tab, in the **Advanced Animation** group, click the **Add Animation** button, and then at the bottom of the gallery, click the animation category you want.

2. In the **Change *Animation* Effect** dialog box, click the animation you want.

➤ **To preview the animation for a selected object**

→ On the **Animations** tab, in the **Preview** group, click the **Preview** button.

➤ **To remove an animation from a selected object**

→ In the **Animation** gallery, click **None**.

➤ **To apply additional animation to a selected animated object**

→ On the **Animations** tab, in the **Advanced Animation** group, click the **Add Animation** button, and then click the additional animation you want to apply.

➤ **To copy the animations applied to a selected object to another object**

→ In the **Advanced Animation** group, click the **Animation Painter** button, and then click the object to which you want to copy the animations.

➤ **To change the order of the selected animation**

→ On the **Animations** tab, in the **Reorder Animation** area of the **Timing** group, click **Move Earlier** or **Move Later**.

> **Tip** You can also change the order of animations in the Animation pane. For information about the Animation pane, animation triggers, and animation timings, see section 4.3, "Set timing for transitions and animations."

Modify animation effects

The animation names reflect the basic action of each animation. After you apply an animation effect, you can fine-tune its action by using the commands on the Animations tab. Depending on the basic action of the animation and the element you are animating, you can configure one or more of the following settings for an animation:

- Amount
- Color
- Direction
- Number of spokes
- Sequence
- Shape
- Vanishing point

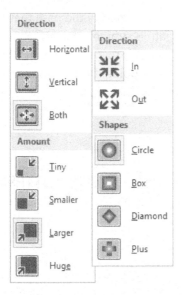

The available effect options vary based on the specific animation. Many animations, such as Appear/Disappear, Fade, Grow & Turn/Shrink & Turn, Swivel, Bounce, Pulse, Teeter, Desaturate, Darken, and Lighten don't have effect options when applied to individual objects, but you can customize other aspects of the animation such as the associated sound, the action of the object after the animation finishes, and the timing aspects such as trigger, duration, and delay.

➤ **To select an animation for further configuration**

→ On the slide, click the animation number.

→ In the **Animation** pane, click the animation number or description.

➤ **To configure basic effect options for a selected animation**

→ In the **Animation** group, click the **Effect Options** button, and then click the option you want.

➤ **To configure advanced effect options for a selected animation**

→ In the **Animation** pane, right-click the animation, click **Effect Options**, and then on the **Effect** page of the *Animation* dialog box, configure the **Sound**, **After animation**, and other available effects.

Configure motion paths

After you apply a Motion Path animation, you can modify the path that the animation follows. Regardless of whether the motion path is straight, shaped, or curved, it has a start point (a green triangle), a rotation handle, and sizing handles. If a motion path is straight or curved, and doesn't return to its start point, it also has an end point (a red triangle). You can adjust the path by using any of these tools.

Dragging the start point or end point displays the animated objects in both positions. If smart guides are turned on (which they are by default), you can use them to align the animated object with other slide elements.

It is important to note that you can move the animated object independent of its motion path so that the object moves from its original location on the slide to the beginning of the motion path, before following the motion path.

➤ **To adjust the height or length of the motion path of a selected animation**

→ Drag the top, bottom, side, or corner handles.

➤ **To change the shape of the motion path of a selected animation**

→ On the **Animations** tab, in the **Animation** group, in the **Effect Options** list, click the shape you want.

➤ **To rotate the motion path of a selected animation**

→ Drag the rotation handle in a circular motion.

➤ **To begin a motion path in a location other than the object location**

→ Drag the object away from the start point of the motion path.

→ Drag the start point of the motion path away from the object.

Practice tasks

The practice file for these tasks is located in the MOSPowerPoint2013\Objective4 practice file folder. Save the results of the tasks in the same folder.

- Open the *PowerPoint_4-2* presentation, and then complete the following tasks:
  - On slide 1, apply the Fly In entrance animation to the slide title, configure it to fly in from the left side of the slide, and then attach the Breeze sound to the animation.
  - On slide 2, apply the Appear entrance animation to the title, and the Pulse emphasis animation to the bulleted list. Then make the color of each bullet point change to green after it appears on the screen.
  - Copy the animations from slide 2 to the corresponding elements on slide 3.
  - On slide 4, apply a different emphasis animation to each of the four pictures in the content area. Then configure a Custom Path motion path animation that causes the ladybug to walk to the lower-left corner of the slide, around the other insects and animals.
- Display the presentation in Slide Show view to test your work.

4.3 Set timing for transitions and animations

When you are incorporating slide transitions and animations into a presentation, two of the options you have for each of these are triggers and timing.

The trigger is the event that causes a transition or animation to begin. The default trigger for a transition or animation is On Mouse Click, meaning that the effect occurs when the presenter gives the signal to advance. When a slide includes animations that are set to start On Mouse Click, the signal to advance the slide instead runs the animation.

The timing of transitions and animations contributes to the tone of a presentation, particularly when the presentation is running automatically. All timing options can be entered in seconds but are expressed in the format *hh:mm:ss*.

Set timing for transitions

The timing options for transitions are in the Timing group on the Transitions tab. The Advance Slide options govern the time at or after which PowerPoint moves to the next slide. There are two Advance Slide options: On Mouse Click and After (which you set to a specific length of time). One or both of these options can be selected. If you plan to deliver a presentation in person, it is customary to retain the On Mouse Click trigger, and to advance the slide manually. Selecting the After check box and specifying a length of time causes PowerPoint to automatically transition to the next slide after that time interval. Selecting both check boxes permits the presenter to manually advance the slide before the specified time has elapsed.

The length of time from the beginning to the end of a transition effect is its duration. A short duration results in the full slide content appearing quickly, and a long duration results in it appearing slowly. Factors to consider when setting the duration include the type of content on the slide and the selected transition. For example, you might want to assign a short duration to a slide transition for which the slide content is not visible until the transition completes. You might assign a long duration to a transition that causes the slide content to appear in legible segments while you discuss it. PowerPoint recognizes the wait time required for various transition effects to deliver legible slide content; for this reason, the default transition duration varies based on the transition.

➤ **To manually trigger the transition to the next slide**

→ On the **Transitions** tab, in the **Timing** group, select the **On Mouse Click** check box.

➤ **To automate the transition of the selected slide**

1. On the **Transitions** tab, in the **Timing** group, below **Advance Slide,** clear the **On Mouse Click** check box.

2. Select the **After** check box, and then enter a time in the adjacent box.

➤ **To change the speed of the transition of a selected slide**

→ In the **Timing** group, enter the number of seconds you want the transition to continue in the **Duration** box.

> **See Also** For more information about slide timings, see section 1.5, "Configure and present slide shows."

Set timing for animations

The timing options for animations are in the Timing group on the Animations tab. Three timing options can be configured for each animation: Start, Duration, and Delay. The timing options are also expressed visually in the Animation pane.

There are three Start options: On Click, With Previous, and With Next. On Click runs the animation when the presenter gives the signal to advance, or clicks a specific trigger object on the slide. With Previous starts the animation at the same time as the preceding animation (or in the case of the first animation, immediately after the slide appears). With Next runs the animation and starts the next animation or action when the presenter gives the signal. The most common use for this setting is to run the final animation on the slide and then immediately transition to the next slide.

As with transitions, the Duration is the length of time from the beginning to the end of an animation effect. The Delay is the length of time PowerPoint waits after the trigger signal to play the animation.

➤ **To manually trigger a selected animation**

1. On the **Animations** tab, in the **Timing** group, in the **Start** list, click **On Click**.

2. To trigger the animation by clicking a specific object, in the **Advanced Animation** group, click **Trigger**, click **On Click of**, and then click the trigger object.

➤ **To automate the start of the selected animation**

→ In the **Timing** group, in the **Start** list, click **With Previous**.

➤ **To automate the action after the selected animation**

→ In the **Timing** group, in the **Start** list, click **After Previous**.

➤ **To change the duration of an animation**

→ In the **Timing** group, enter the number of seconds you want the animation to continue in the **Duration** box.

➤ **To delay the start of an animation**

→ In the **Timing** group, enter the number of seconds you want to delay the animation in the **Delay** box.

Manage animations in the Animation pane

The Animation pane displays a visual description of the animation sequence occurring on a slide.

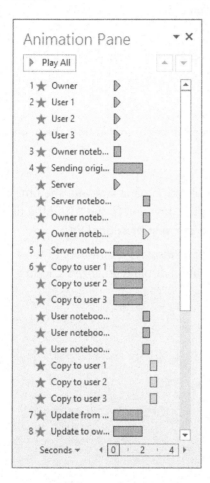

Several information points are visible for each animation:

- The number (corresponding to the number next to the animated object on the slide) indicates the order in which a manually triggered animation occurs. An unnumbered animation starts in relation to the numbered animation it follows.

- The icon indicates the animation category. A green star indicates an entrance effect, a yellow star indicates an emphasis effect, a red star indicates an exit effect, and a blue double-ended line indicates a motion path. The specific animation is not indicated by the icon.

- The description indicates the object being animated.

> **Tip** Object names can be edited in the Selection pane. For information about the Selection pane, see section 2.3, "Order and group shapes and slides."

- The Advanced Timeline displays a triangle or bar that indicates the duration of the animation. The color of the triangle or bar corresponds to the animation category (green, yellow, red, or blue).

> **Tip** The display of the Advanced Timeline can be controlled from the Animation pane object shortcut menu.

- The timing bar at the bottom of the Animation pane indicates the time scale. The time scale can be modified by clicking the time unit to the left of the timing bar (Seconds, by default) and then clicking Zoom In or Zoom Out.

Pointing to an animation in the Animation pane displays a summary of the animation information in a ScreenTip. Clicking an animation displays an arrow. Clicking the arrow displays a list of actions.

Clicking Effect Options in the list displays a dialog box that is specific to that type of animation.

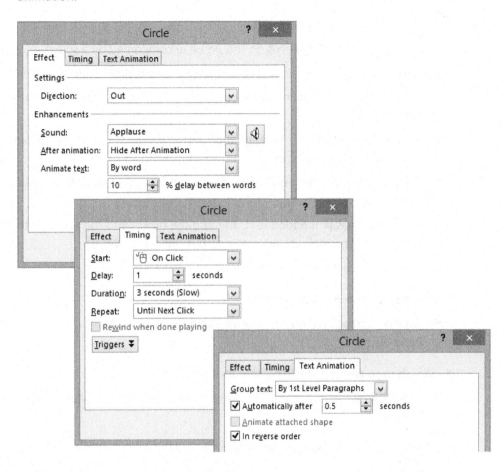

Depending on the type of animation, the refinements you might be able to make include the following:

- Change the animation direction.
- Specify whether the animation should be accompanied by a sound.
- Dim or hide the object after the animation, or make it change to a specific color.
- If the animation is applied to text, animate all the text at once, word by word, or letter by letter.
- Change the Start, Delay, and Duration settings, repeat the animation, and specify what will trigger its action.
- If a slide has more than one level of bullet points, animate different levels separately.
- If an object has embedded text, animate the object and the text together (the default) or separately, or animate one but not the other.
- Specify whether a sequenced animation progresses forward or backward.

➤ **To display the Animation pane**

➜ On the **Animations** tab, in the **Advanced Animation** group, click the **Animation Pane** button.

➤ **To change the order of the selected animation**

➜ In the upper-right corner of the **Animation** pane, click the **Move Earlier** or **Move Later** arrow.

➤ **To display the Effect Options dialog box for an animation**

➜ In the **Animation** pane, click the animation, click the arrow that appears, and then click **Effect Options**.

➤ **To add sound to an animation**

➜ On the **Effect** page of the **Effect Options** dialog box, in the **Sound** list, click the sound you want.

➤ **To dim, hide, or change the color of text or an object after its animation completes**

→ On the **Effect** page of the **Effect Options** dialog box, in the **After animation** list, click the color or effect you want.

➤ **To animate text by container, by word, or by letter**

→ On the **Effect** page of the **Effect Options** dialog box, in the **Animate text** list, click **All at once**, **By word**, or **By letter**.

➤ **To set the animation trigger**

→ On the **Timing** page of the **Effect Options** dialog box, in the **Start** list, click **On Click**, **With Previous**, or **With Next**.

➤ **To set the delay of an animation**

→ On the **Timing** page of the **Effect Options** dialog box, in the **Delay** box, enter the delay in seconds.

➤ **To set the duration of an animation (limited options)**

→ On the **Timing** page of the **Effect Options** dialog box, in the **Duration** list, click **5 seconds (Very Slow)**, **3 seconds (Slow)**, **2 seconds (Medium)**, **1 seconds (Fast)**, or **0.5 seconds (Very Fast)**.

> **Tip** A duration other than one of those in the list can be set in the Timing group on the Animations tab.

➤ **To set the grouping of multiple paragraphs of animated text**

→ On the **Text Animation** page of the **Effect Options** dialog box, display the **Group text** list, and then click **As One Object**, **All Paragraphs At Once**, or the paragraph level by which you want to group the text.

➤ **To change the order in which text is animated**

→ On the **Text Animation** page of the **Effect Options** dialog box, select the **In reverse order** check box.

Practice tasks

The practice file for these tasks is located in the MOSPowerPoint2013\Objective4 practice file folder. Save the results of the tasks in the same folder.

● Open the *PowerPoint_4-3* presentation, and then complete the following tasks:

○ On slide 1, make the subtitle animation start automatically after the title animation, with a delay of 2 seconds.

○ On slide 2, set the duration of the bulleted list animations to 2 seconds. Then make the title animation occur after the bulleted list animations.

○ On slide 4, set the slide title to animate word by word, with a 50 percent delay between words and a duration of Very Slow. Then change the order of the animations to frog, butterfly, ladybug, bee, and then mouse.

Objective review

Before finishing this chapter, ensure that you have mastered the following skills:

4.1   Apply transitioning between slides

4.2   Animate slide content

4.3   Set timing for transitions and animations

5 Manage multiple presentations

The skills tested in this section of the Microsoft Office Specialist exam for Microsoft PowerPoint 2013 relate to collaborating with other people on presentations. Specifically, the following objectives are associated with this set of skills:

5.1 Merge content from multiple presentations

5.2 Track changes and resolve differences

5.3 Protect and share presentations

When working with colleagues to develop a presentation, you might each develop a separate part of the presentation and then merge the presentations into one, or you might work in multiple versions of the whole presentation and then merge those into one. During the collaboration process, it is frequently necessary to review changes made by one or more people and decide which version of the content to retain.

When you and your colleagues need to communicate about a presentation that you're developing, one method of doing so is by inserting information in comments attached to specific slides or slide content.

This chapter guides you in studying ways of reusing content from one presentation in another, merging multiple versions of a presentation, comparing differences and accepting or rejecting changes, and managing comments.

> **Practice Files** To complete the practice tasks in this chapter, you need the practice files contained in the MOSPowerPoint2013\Objective5 practice file folder. For more information, see "Download the practice files" in this book's Introduction.

5.1 Merge content from multiple presentations

Display multiple presentations

Each PowerPoint presentation you open is displayed in its own program window. As a result, you can not only switch among open presentations, but you can also view multiple presentations simultaneously. You can display windows side by side or in a cascading arrangement so that you can easily click the one you want.

When you want to view two different parts of the same presentation, you can open a second instance of the presentation in a separate window, arrange the windows side by side, and then scroll the windows independently. (In fact, you can open many instances of a presentation.) Each window is identified in the title bar by the instance number after the file name.

➤ **To view more than one presentation at the same time**

→ On the **View** tab, in the **Window** group, click the **Arrange All** button to arrange the open program windows side by side.

→ In the **Window** group, click the **Cascade** button to arrange the open program windows in an overlapping formation.

➤ **To view different parts of the same presentation**

→ On the **View** tab, in the **Window** group, click the **New Window** button. Then arrange the open windows, and scroll to the parts of the presentation you want to display in each window.

Reuse slides from other presentations

If you want to reuse the slides from one presentation in another, you can easily do so. You can reuse slides directly from one presentation in another, but if you know in advance that you will want to reuse a slide, you can publish it to the slide library on your computer and then reuse it from there, without having to track down the presentation or undo any presentation-specific modifications that you might have made to the slide.

You can manually copy slides from one presentation to another, but PowerPoint provides a more sophisticated method of doing this, in the Reuse Slides pane.

CHIN
SUS
xxxxxxx5100
.
1/27/2018

Item: 0010086787792 ((book)

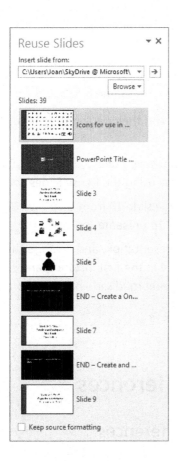

> **To reuse slides from a saved presentation**

1. In the **Thumbnails** pane or **Slide Sorter** pane, click where you want to insert the reused slide or slides.

2. On the **Home** tab or **Insert** tab, in the **Slides** group, click the **New Slide** arrow, and then click **Reuse Slides**.

3. In the **Reuse Slides** pane, click **Browse**, and then click **Browse File**.

4. In the **Browse** dialog box, locate and double-click the presentation containing the slides you want to reuse.

5. In the **Reuse Slides** pane, click each slide you want to reuse, and then close the pane.

Tip By default, reused slides take on the formatting of the presentation into which they are inserted. To retain the slides' source formatting, select the Keep Source Formatting check box before inserting the first slide.

Practice tasks

The practice files for these tasks are located in the MOSPowerPoint2013\Objective5 practice file folder. Save the results of the tasks in the same folder.

- Open the *PowerPoint_5-1a* presentation, and then perform the following tasks:

  - After slide 4, merge slide 5 from the *PowerPoint_5-1b* presentation into the *PowerPoint_5-1a* presentation by using the Reuse Slides command.

  - At the end of the presentation, merge slide 10 from the *PowerPoint_5-1b* presentation into the *PowerPoint_5-1a* presentation.

  - Display a second instance of the presentation, and arrange the two instances side by side. Display slide 4 in the first instance, and slide 5 in the second instance. Ensure that the merged slide has taken on the formatting of the presentation.

5.2 Track changes and resolve differences

Compare, combine, and review differences

> **Strategy** Viewing, accepting, and rejecting revisions in PowerPoint is not as intuitive as it is in Microsoft Word. Take some time to practice making changes to a presentation and comparing it with the original version to become familiar with ways of working with this feature.

You can compare two versions of the same presentation by merging changes made in one version into the other. The differences are recorded in the combined presentation as revisions. You can view the suggested changes and then accept or reject them.

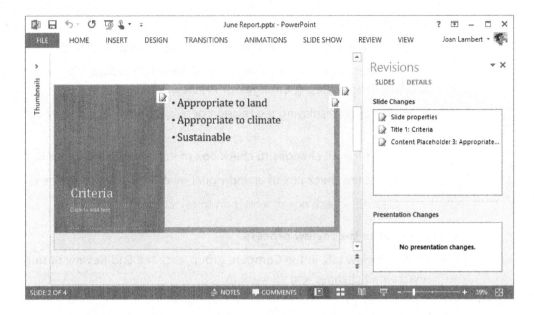

> ➤ **To combine two versions of the same presentation**

1. With one version open, on the **Review** tab, in the **Compare** group, click the **Compare** button.

2. In the **Choose File to Merge with Current Presentation** dialog box, locate and double-click the version you want to combine.

> ➤ **To review revisions**

→ On the slide, click any revision icon to display revision details.

   Or

1. In the **Revisions** pane (which opens automatically after you combine two versions), display the **Details** page.

2. In the **Slide Changes** box, click any revision to display details.

3. On the **Review** tab, in the **Compare** group, click the **Next** button to move to the next slide with changes.

   Or

1. In the **Revisions** pane, display the **Slides** page.

2. In the **Thumbnails** pane, click any slide to display the original version in the content pane and the modified version in the **Revisions** pane.

➤ **To accept or reject revisions**

➜ On the **Review** tab, in the **Compare** group, click **Accept** or **Reject**.

➜ On the **Slides** page of the **Revisions** pane, point to a revised slide, and then click **Accept Changes**, **Reject Changes**, or **Preview**.

➜ In the ScreenTip displaying the revision details for an object, do any of the following:

  ○ Select the **All changes to** check box to implement all changes to the object.

  ○ Select the check box of an individual revision to implement the change.

  ○ Clear the check box of a revision to reject the change.

➤ **To complete the review process**

➜ On the **Review** tab, in the **Compare** group, click the **End Review** button to discard unaccepted changes and all markup.

> **Tip** To accept changes without displaying the details, on the Review tab, in the Compare group, click the Accept arrow, and then click Accept All Changes To This Slide or Accept All Changes To The Presentation. If you change your mind, in the Compare group, click the Reject arrow, and then click Reject All Changes To This Slide or Reject All Changes To The Presentation.

Manage comments

If you are asked to review a presentation, you can give feedback about a slide, without disrupting its text and layout, by inserting a comment. If you add a comment without first selecting an object on the slide, a small comment icon appears in the upper-left corner of the slide. If you select an object before adding the comment, the comment icon appears in the upper-right corner of the object.

You add comments in the Comments pane, where comments are identified by the user name specified on the General page of the PowerPoint Options dialog box. You can work with the Comments pane open, or close it until you need it again.

Closing the Comments pane leaves the comment icons on the slide. Clicking a comment icon opens the Comments pane and displays the selected comment.

You can turn the display of comments on and off and move quickly back and forth among the comments by using the commands in the Comments group on the Review tab. You can reply to comments to create a focused conversation about a slide or slide object. You can delete comments individually, delete all the comments on a slide, or delete all the comments in a presentation.

➤ **To insert a comment**

1. Click the slide or object on the slide to which you want to attach a comment.

2. On the **Review** tab, in the **Comments** group, click the **New Comment** button.

3. In the **Comments** pane, enter the comment in the box that opens.

➤ **To display and hide the Comments pane**

→ On the **Review** tab, in the **Comments** group, click the **Show Markup** button.

→ Click a comment icon to display the comment.

→ Click the **Close** button in the upper-right corner of the **Comments** pane to close the pane.

➤ **To move among comments**

→ In the **Comments** pane, click the **Previous** or **Next** button.

→ On the **Review** tab, in the **Comments** group, click the **Previous** or **Next** button.

➤ **To edit a comment**

→ In the **Comments** pane, click the comment, and then modify the text.

➤ **To reply to a comment**

→ In the **Comments** pane, click the **Reply** box for the comment, and then enter your reply.

➤ **To delete a specific comment**

→ Right-click the comment icon, and then click **Delete Comment**.

→ Click the comment icon, and then on the **Review** tab, in the **Comments** group, click the **Delete** button.

→ In the **Comments** pane, point to the comment, and then click the **Delete** button that appears.

➤ **To delete all the comments on the current slide**

→ On the **Review** tab, in the **Comments** group, click the **Delete** arrow, and then click **Delete All Comments on This Slide**.

➤ **To delete all the comments in the presentation**

1. On the **Review** tab, in the **Comments** group, click the **Delete** arrow, and then click **Delete All Comments in This Presentation**.

2. To confirm the deletion, click **Yes**.

Practice tasks

The practice files for these tasks are located in the MOSPowerPoint2013\Objective5 practice file folder. Save the results of the tasks in the same folder.

* Open the *PowerPoint_5-2a* and *PowerPoint_5-2b* presentations, and merge the differences into *PowerPoint_5-2b*.

* Review the marked differences, accept those on slide 1, and then reject all other changes.

* Open the *PowerPoint_5-2c* presentation, and then perform the following tasks:

  ○ In the header of slide 2, insert the comment *Change date to reflect that of workshop.*

  ○ On slide 9, attach the comment *Newer data available?* to the citation.

  ○ On slide 13, attach the comment *Native plant graphics would add interest* to the content placeholder. Click away from the comment to close the box, and then edit it to read *Colorful native plant graphics would add interest.*

* Open the *PowerPoint_5-2d* presentation, and then perform the following tasks:

  ○ Delete the comments attached to the title slide.

  ○ Review the remaining comments in the presentation.

  ○ Using only one command, delete all the remaining comments.

5.3 Protect and share presentations

Proof presentations

The AutoCorrect feature detects and automatically corrects many common capitalization and spelling errors, such as *teh* instead of *the* or *WHen* instead of *When*. You can customize AutoCorrect to recognize words you frequently misspell.

> **Tip** You can also use AutoCorrect entries to automate the typing of frequently used text, such as replacing an abbreviation of a company name with the full name of the company.

By default, PowerPoint checks the spelling of anything you enter against its built-in dictionary. To draw attention to a word that is not in its dictionary and that might be misspelled, PowerPoint underlines it with a red wavy underline.

> **Tip** To turn off the display of red wavy lines, clear the Check Spelling As You Type check box on the Proofing page of the PowerPoint Options dialog box.

You can correct the marked spelling errors immediately or ignore the red wavy underlines and instead handle all the potential misspellings in the presentation at one time by clicking options in the Spelling pane.

You can add correctly spelled words that are flagged as misspellings to the supplemental dictionary so that PowerPoint will not flag them in the future.

> **To add an entry and its replacement to the AutoCorrect list**

1. On the **Proofing** page of the **PowerPoint Options** dialog box, in the **AutoCorrect options** area, click the **AutoCorrect Options** button.

2. On the **AutoCorrect** page of the **AutoCorrect** dialog box, enter the misspelling in the **Replace** box.

3. Enter the correction in the **With** box.

4. Click **Add**, and then click **OK**.

> **To correct a word that is marked by a red wavy underline**

→ Right-click the word, and then click the suggested replacement you want.

➤ **To check the spelling of the entire presentation at one time**

1. On the **Review** tab, in the **Proofing** group, click the **Spelling** button.

2. For each word PowerPoint flags, do one of the following in the **Spelling** pane:

- ○ To ignore the flagged word, click **Ignore** or **Ignore All**.

- ○ To change the flagged word, click a suggested correction, or enter the correction in the **Change to** box. Then click either **Change** or **Change All**.

- ○ To delete a duplicated word, click **Delete**.

- ○ To add a word to the supplemental dictionary, click **Add**.

Inspect presentations

Presentations are often delivered electronically, as attachments to email messages or as files that can be downloaded from a website.

If your presentation might be delivered as a file to people who are using an earlier version of PowerPoint, you can inspect the presentation by running the Compatibility Checker, to identify any elements that won't display or perform as expected in that version.

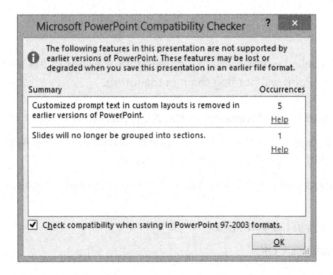

Before distributing a presentation, you will want to remove the identifying and tracking properties that were attached by PowerPoint while the presentation was being developed. These properties include information such as the author's name, the title, and when the file was created and updated. You might also have attached other properties, such as keywords.

To ensure that all properties are removed, you can use the Document Inspector feature, which can also flag and remove items such as comments, notes, and other content that you might not want to distribute.

Many organizations choose to or must comply with international accessibility standards that are designed to ensure that information in computer-based communications can be accurately interpreted by devices such as screen readers. The Accessibility Checker provides information about presentation elements that might not be correctly interpreted.

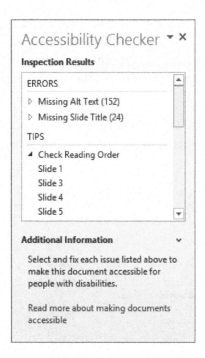

➤ **To check for compatibility with previous versions of PowerPoint**

→ On the **Info** page of the **Backstage** view, click **Check for Issues**, and then click **Check Compatibility**.

➤ **To remove information before distributing a presentation**

1. On the **Info** page of the **Backstage** view, click **Check for Issues**, and then click **Inspect Document**.

2. In the **Document Inspector** dialog box, clear the check boxes for types of information you don't want to locate, and then click **Inspect**.

3. When the Document Inspector reports its findings, click **Remove All** for any type of information you want to remove.

➤ **To check for accessibility issues**

1. On the **Info** page of the **Backstage** view, click **Check for Issues**, and then click **Check Accessibility**.

2. In the **Inspection Results** pane, click any header to display a list of slides to which the error or tip pertains.

3. In the **Inspection Results** pane, click any slide to display that slide.

Protect presentations

The simplest way to control access to a presentation is to assign a password to it. You can assign two types of passwords:

- **Password to open** Assigning this type of password encrypts the presentation so that only people with the password can open and view it.

- **Password to modify** Assigning this type of password does not encrypt the presentation. Users can open the presentation in read-only mode or enter a password to open the presentation in edit mode.

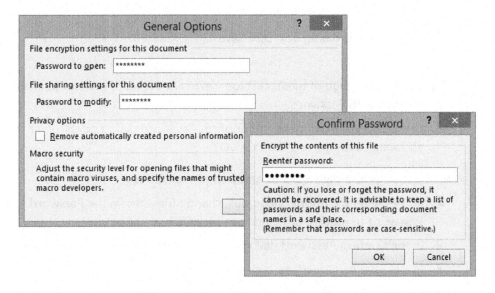

> **Tip** You can also assign a password to open a presentation from the Info page of the Backstage view.

To open a presentation that requires a password to open, you must enter the exact password, including capitalization, numbers, spaces, and symbols. To open a presentation that requires a password only to modify, you can either enter the exact password to open and modify it or open a version that you can view but not modify.

➤ **To set a password for a presentation**

1. In the **Save As** dialog box, click the **Tools** button, and then click **General Options**.

2. In the **General Options** dialog box, in the **Password to open** or **Password to modify** box, enter the password you want, and then click **OK**.

3. In the **Confirm Password** dialog box, reenter the password you previously entered, and then click **OK**.

> **Tip** In the General Options dialog box, you can enter both passwords. In that case, you will be asked to confirm each in turn.

4. In the **Save As** dialog box, click **Save**.

Or

1. On the **Info** page of the **Backstage** view, click **Protect Presentation**, and then click **Encrypt with Password**.

2. In the **Encrypt Document** and **Confirm Password** dialog boxes, enter the password you want to assign, and then click **OK**.

➤ **To change the password of an open presentation**

1. In the **General Options** dialog box, change the entry in the **Password to open** or **Password to modify** box, and then click **OK**.

2. In the **Confirm Password** dialog box, reenter the new password, and then click **OK**.

3. In the **Save As** dialog box, click **Save**.

Or

1. On the **Info** page of the **Backstage** view, click **Protect Presentation**, and then click **Encrypt with Password**.

2. In the **Encrypt Document** dialog box, change the password, and then click **OK**.

3. In the **Confirm Password** dialog box, reenter the password you entered in the previous step, and then click **OK**.

➤ **To delete the password of an open presentation**

1. In the **General Options** dialog box, delete either or both passwords, and then click **OK**.

2. In the **Save As** dialog box, click **Save**.

    Or

1. On the **Info** page of the **Backstage** view, click **Protect Presentation**, and then click **Encrypt with Password**.

2. In the **Encrypt Document** dialog box, delete the password, and then click **OK**.

Prepare presentations for distribution

Before you share a media-intensive presentation with other people, you might want to compress the media to make the presentation file smaller and more portable. PowerPoint offers three levels of compression.

> **Tip** The Compress Media button appears on the Info page only if the presentation contains audio clips or video clips.

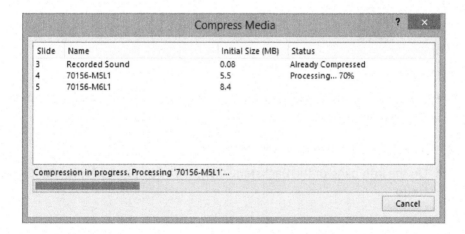

If your presentation uses specialized fonts that might not be available on a viewer's computer, you can embed the fonts in the presentation to ensure that the presentation content appears as you intend it to.

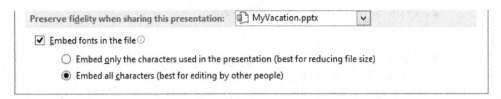

After you finish preparing a presentation for distribution, you can mark it as final. This feature saves the file, deactivates most PowerPoint tools, and displays an information bar at the top of the screen to indicate that no further changes should be made to the presentation. However, you can easily override the final status and make changes to the presentation.

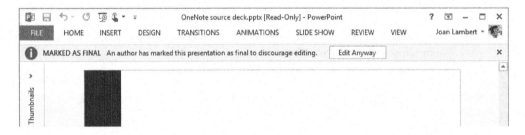

> **To compress media**

→ On the **Info** page of the **Backstage** view, click **Compress Media**, and then click **Presentation Quality**, **Internet Quality**, or **Low Quality**.

> **To reverse a compression operation**

→ On the **Info** page of the **Backstage** view, click **Compress Media**, and then click **Undo**.

➤ **To embed fonts in a presentation**

1. On the **Save** page of the **PowerPoint Options** dialog box, in the **Preserve fidelity when sharing this presentation** section, select the **Embed fonts in the file** check box.

2. Do either of the following, and then click **OK**:

   ○ To embed only the characters that are necessary for the current version of the presentation, click **Embed only the characters used in the presentation**.

   ○ To embed all characters of all fonts that are present in the presentation so that they are available to another person who works with the presentation, click **Embed all characters**.

3. Save the modified presentation, or save a copy of the presentation that is for the express purpose of distribution, and close the smaller original file without saving the changes.

➤ **To mark a presentation as final**

1. On the **Info** page of the **Backstage** view, click **Protect Presentation**, and then click **Mark as Final**.

2. In the message box, click **OK**, and then click **OK** in the confirmation box.

➤ **To turn off the final status**

→ In the information bar below the ribbon, click **Edit Anyway**.

→ On the **Info** page of the **Backstage** view, click the pink-shaded **Protect Presentation** button, and then click **Mark as Final**.

Practice tasks

The practice files for these tasks are located in the MOSPowerPoint2013\Objective5 practice file folder. Save the results of the tasks in the same folder.

- Open the *PowerPoint_5-3a* presentation, and then perform the following tasks:

  - On slide 2, correct the spelling of *infermation*.

  - Check the spelling of the entire presentation, correcting any mistakes you find. Add the term *CSCom* to the dictionary.

  - Add the correct spelling of *employes* to the AutoCorrect substitution table.

- Open the *PowerPoint_5-3b* presentation, and then perform the following tasks:

  - Remove all identifying and tracking information and comments from the file.

  - Assign the password *P@ssword* to the presentation so that the file can be opened but not changed. Then save the presentation with the name *MyPassword*, and close it.

- Open a read-only version of the password-protected *MyPassword* presentation, try to make a change, and then close it. Then open a version you can edit, delete the word *key* in the first two bullets on the last slide, and save the presentation.

- Reopen the *PowerPoint_5-3b* presentation, and mark it as final.

Objective review

Before finishing this chapter, ensure that you have mastered the following skills:

5.1 Merge content from multiple presentations

5.2 Track changes and resolve differences

5.3 Protect and share presentations

Index

F

G

H

I

J

K

About the author

 **Joan Lambert** has worked closely with Microsoft technologies since 1986, and in the training and certification industry since 1997. As President of Online Training Solutions, Inc. (OTSI), Joan is responsible for guiding the translation of technical information and requirements into useful, relevant, and measurable training and certification tools.

Joan is a Microsoft Certified Trainer, Microsoft Office Master, Microsoft Certified Technology Specialist, Microsoft Technology Associate, and the author of more than two dozen books about Windows and Office (for Windows and Mac). Joan enthusiastically shares her love of technology through her participation in the creation of books, learning materials, and certification exams.

Joan currently lives in a nearly perfect small town in Texas with her simply divine daughter, Trinity, two dogs, one cat, a multitude of fish, and the super-automatic espresso machine that runs the house.

Online Training Solutions, Inc. (OTSI)

OTSI specializes in the design, creation, and production of Microsoft Office, SharePoint, and Windows training products for information workers and home computer users. For more information about OTSI, visit *www.otsi.com*.

The team

This book would not exist without the support of these hard-working members of the OTSI publishing team:

- Denise Bankaitis
- Rob Carr
- Susie Carr
- Jeanne Craver

- Kathy Krause
- Marlene Lambert
- Barb Levy
- Jaime Odell

- Victoria Thulman
- Jean Trenary
- Krista Wall

We are especially thankful to the support staff at home who make it possible for our team members to devote their time and attention to these projects.

Rosemary Caperton and Valerie Woolley provided invaluable support on behalf of Microsoft Press.

Now that you've read the book...

Tell us what you think!

Was it useful?
Did it teach you what you wanted to learn?
Was there room for improvement?

Let us know at http://aka.ms/tellpress

Your feedback goes directly to the staff at Microsoft Press,
and we read every one of your responses. Thanks in advance!

 Microsoft

CPSIA information can be obtained
at www.ICGtesting.com
Printed in the USA
LVOW04s2036100118
562547LV00018B/269/P

9 780735 669239